Important: Do not remove this
date due reminder.

DATE DUE

BATTLE OF PEA RIDGE,
ARKANSAS, MARCH 7-8, 1862

BY HERMAN J. VIOLA

Warriors
IN UNIFORM
THE LEGACY OF AMERICAN INDIAN HEROISM

Foreword by
CARSON WALKS OVER ICE
Introduction by
SENATOR BEN NIGHTHORSE CAMPBELL

NATIONAL GEOGRAPHIC

WASHINGTON, D.C.

OUR ENEMIES ARE CRYING

Isshe'ele Uuwateesh Iiweek
The Ones with Metal on the Top of the Head (the Lakota) are crying
Ikku'pe Uuwateesh Iiweek
The Metal Hats (the Germans of World War I and II) are crying
Chee'tbachee Pu'mmeesh Iiweek
The Short Wolf Men (the Asians of World War II, Korea, and Vietnam) are crying
Ishbi'tchia Lu'sshiash Iiweek
The Curved Knives (the Arabs of the Gulf War, Lebanon, Afghanistan, and Iraq) are crying
Alawachee' Waatcha'achik Huuash Iiweek
We heard that he was an outstanding man (the enemy soldier) but he is crying

—Crow Nation Warrior Song

CONTENTS

INTRODUCTION

I am a veteran of the Korean War and I am also an American Indian, a member of the Cheyenne Nation. We are a warrior people. We are proud of our military heritage and our country and, like our fellow native brothers and sisters in uniform, we will always be in the front ranks when our nation needs us, which is only right since we are the "first" Americans.

We had lived in this wonderful country for thousands of years before Christopher Columbus arrived in the "New World" in 1492 and mistakenly called us Indians because he thought he was in India. That is why we are called Indians. I can speak for all Native Americans when I tell you we are sure happy Columbus did not think he was in Turkey.

No matter. Though we may be of different ethnic groups in this country, we are still of one family, and that is the American family. Indeed, to this day I can remember the feeling I had as our troop ship returned to port in San Francisco in the spring of 1952. We had stayed on deck throughout the night just so we could see the Golden Gate emerge through the morning fog. I was only a 19-year-old airman at the time and yet my memory of the pride and love of country we all felt on board that ship are as clear today as they were over a half century ago.

As you will learn from this book, the relationship between American Indians and the modern U.S. military, with a few historic exceptions, has been a strong one. I say a few exceptions because there was a time when some of our Indian people were in an adversarial position with the U.S. military. The Seneca Nation, for example, burned and sank three U.S. naval warships during the War of 1812, and my Cheyenne people did not welcome George Armstrong Custer and the Seventh Cavalry with open arms in 1876.

Nonetheless, American Indians have proudly worn our nation's uniform in every one of our conflicts. In fact, as early as 1778 our country enlisted the services of Native Americans, both as scouts and as light infantry. Indians fought the British with Andrew Jackson at the Battle of New Orleans during the War of 1812, and they proudly wore the uniforms of the North and South in our nation's Civil War, which was a civil war for many of our Indian tribes as well. They served with Black Jack Pershing when he chased the Mexican bandit Pancho Villa into Mexico. They were with Teddy Roosevelt's Rough Riders as they charged up San Juan Hill. Twelve thousand Native Americans saw action in WWI, even though they could not even vote in the United States until 1924. Forty-four thousand Native American "citizens" served in WWII. I have never known a Native American who has vacationed on the beaches of the Riviera, but I have known many who shed their blood on the beaches of Anzio and Normandy, on Inchon and Iwo Jima.

The bond between Indian nations and the U.S. military has been and remains strong. Moreover, warriors do not need to be drafted; they step forward when duty calls. American Indians—per capita—have had the highest percentage of their people in military service, exceeding every American ethnic group. Today there are over 13,000 American Indians on active duty serving our country across the world. And thanks to this book, their 200 years of selfless patriotism, loyalty, and sacrifice to our country has finally been recognized and acknowledged.

—Ben Nighthorse Campbell
Former U.S. Senator
Colorado

RON HAWKS OF THE LAKOTA
NATION PERFORMS FOR
THE SOLDIERS DURING
NATIVE HERITAGE MONTH AT
HOHENFELS, GERMANY.

FOREWORD

My name is Carson Walks Over Ice, and I am a member of the Crow Nation of Montana. My Indian name, Buffalo Chief, was given to me by my clan uncle. All the Crows have a second name in addition to their legal name. You get it from your clan uncle. The name is not for anything that you've done; it is whatever the clan uncle did and wants to give you. My clan uncle gave me his name, Buffalo Chief.

When you give away your name, you need to get another one. It is important to have a second name because the Great Spirit will not know you if you do not have a name. For example, my father-in-law came to me because he had no name. He had given his second name to a grandchild, so he needed a new name and asked me for one. He was afraid that if he died, he wouldn't be known in the spirit world. Because I was in the Army and wore a military patch with an eagle on my shoulder, I gave him the name Eagle Soldier.

I got my second name, Buffalo Chief, when I was in high school because my grandmother thought it was time for me to have another name before I left for the Army. When I was just a little boy, my second name was Flies Through the Clouds. My grandfather was wounded in the Second World War, and the Army brought him back on an airplane that flew through the clouds, so that's how I got that name. I later gave that name to my second son.

I grew up hearing war stories, but in a different way from most people in America. When I was a little guy, my grandfather George Hogan would invite people to his house to tell stories. In those days, we didn't have things like televisions—even radios—so our entertainment was stories about the old days before life on reservations. We would bring people into our homes to tell stories. We would hear about the Crow scouts who helped the cavalry like at the Battle of the Little Bighorn. We would hear the old warriors tell how they fought the Sioux, the Blackfeet, and the Shoshone. They would tell us their war deeds, how they stole horses from the other tribes. For example, my grandfather's second name was Along the Hillside, and his honor song says how he went to an enemy lodge and cut a horse from out front and took it away.

Those warriors had a tradition of defending their people, of defending their lands from the different tribes. And when those old men danced, we heard their honor songs. As little boys we would say to each other that we would do the same thing, we would defend our people. In this way the Crow people pass on their warrior tradition from generation to generation.

All of those stories of war deeds came down to me, and my relatives would say, "This is what your dad did, this is what your uncles did, this is what your brothers did. All of them went to war and they did all of these war deeds."

So when it came my time to serve, I enlisted. Even though my own grandfather was a prisoner of war of the United States during the Indian wars, even with that, I still held a thing for the United States in my heart saying—hey, it's my turn. And despite my fear of heights, I joined the 101st Airborne Ranger Division, the "Screaming Eagles," and became a paratrooper. I was able to jump out of airplanes and helicopters, to land and attack enemy camps. I did all these things for almost ten months before I got wounded and was taken out. But when I came back from Vietnam, I could say to the other veterans, "I did all the stuff that our forefathers did, that you did, that my dad, my uncles, my grandfathers did. I did those things, too."

The Crow, like all our Native American brethren, honor their veterans. Today, when a Crow soldier returns from Iraq or Afghanistan, the family hosts a welcome home ceremony at the Billings (Montana) Airport (see page 204). The family members paint their faces and sing an honor song to the returned warrior, who is given a feathered war bonnet as part of the ceremony. Each family has its own special way of painting their faces. In the old days a special honor song was only for returning wounded warriors. The warriors, who were brought back into camp on horseback at sunrise, were serenaded with this song, which praised their strength compared with the weakness of their enemies.

The Crow tribe has recently revived this ceremony, which is called Welcoming the Warrior Back Into Camp. A special song is now used to honor all Crow soldiers returning from Iraq and Afghanistan, whether wounded or not. This is done to encourage them and to show them that their family respects and appreciates the sacrifices they have made for their country and their people.

Before the present conflicts in Iraq and Afghanistan, the last time the Welcoming the Warrior Back Into Camp ceremony was performed was in 1970 when Eddie Little Light and I returned home from Vietnam. Both of us had been wounded. The ceremony was performed during Crow Fair (an annual gathering and celebration in Montana). Our faces were painted and we were wearing eagle feather war bonnets and buckskins. As we were led into camp on horseback at sunrise, we were followed by friends and relatives, including our mothers and grandmothers, wearing special clothes. Many people witnessed this moving and beautiful ceremony.

Although I had received numerous citations from the U.S. Army for my combat service in Vietnam, I valued more the honors accorded me by my Crow people for upholding our tribe's warrior tradition. In Vietnam I had done my war deeds. I had counted coup on the enemy.

To the Crow people, a war deed is something that says you are a man, that you have faced the enemy. It says that you have heard the gunfire and that you went and did a brave deed in front of the enemy—you are a warrior. We call these war deeds coups. If you accomplish a war deed, we say you have counted coup on the enemy. I guess it comes from the French phrase *coup d'etat,* "to strike."

To become a Crow chief you have to accomplish four different coups. One is to touch an enemy in battle without hurting him—you just reach out and touch him and let him go. The second one is to take an enemy's weapon away from him in battle, again doing it without hurting him. The third coup is to lead a successful war party. This means you have accomplished your objective without any of your men getting hurt. The fourth coup is to cut a horse from in front of an enemy lodge. When you do those four things you are held up in esteem in front of your people. As a paratrooper in Vietnam, I counted many coups.

Counting coup is not about killing the enemy; it is about demonstrating bravery, like the time I reached out and grabbed a Viet Cong soldier who was rushing past me through heavy brush trying to escape from a firefight. As he went past me, I reached out and grabbed him and then said, "Go" in Vietnamese. He just looked at me real funny, and then he ran. I can tell you he was one surprised fellow.

In another fight I pulled a Viet Cong soldier's weapon out of his hands. It was a Russian-made SKS carbine, and I used it the rest of my time in Vietnam. I grabbed the carbine and told him to go, so he ran and he ran.

"Why didn't you kill him?" the white soldiers with me asked. "I had my reasons," I told them, "but you saw me do it and that's all that matters."

My third deed, leading a successful war party, I accomplished many times. My war parties were the endless patrols—search and destroy missions—we conducted in Vietnam. As a platoon leader, I led a bunch of those patrols and did not lose a single soldier, but it was impossible for me to capture an enemy horse because the Viet Cong did not have any. Instead of horses they had elephants, and I did capture four of those.

It was early in the war and the North Vietnamese sometimes used elephants to carry supplies into South Vietnam along the Ho Chi Minh Trail. I was sitting on a ridge overlooking the trail one day when a Viet Cong supply column came along. It was led by a young boy. I didn't realize he was young because he was wearing a helmet and carried an AK-47. After I shot him I spotted these elephants behind him. I grabbed the rope of the lead elephant, but he kept moving. He dragged me for about 100 yards before he finally stopped. The only reason that elephant stopped was that he decided to stop. I had nothing to do with it, but when he stopped I wrapped his rope around a tree. Since he was tied to three other elephants, I can say I captured those four elephants. But they weren't horses, so the old people at home did not count them.

Because of my own combat experiences, I have been anxious to help tell the story of all Indians who have served in our country's armed forces. The telling of that story has been long overdue, and that is why I welcomed the opportunity to help with this book. Their military contributions, their sacrifices to help preserve American democracy deserve recognition. They are the forgotten heroes in this country's history. Few non-Indians are even aware that Native American men and women have served in the ranks of the U.S. military in every one of our nation's wars including our present conflicts in Iraq and Afghanistan. The sad reality is that most of these soldiers, who have come from every tribe in this country, have been "invisible."

What is even more shameful is that American Indians were not citizens of the United States until after World War I. These brave American Indian men and women went into harm's way without ever receiving appropriate recognition for their selfless contributions and service except from their own people.

Even after they obtained citizenship in 1924, Native American men and women may have been welcomed as soldiers on our nation's battlefields, but they remained second-class citizens in their own country regardless of the fact that many of them bled and died on those battlefields. Despite past injustices, our young men and women still choose to enlist and serve their country in numbers that exceed the percentage of any other ethnic group in America because we love this country.

About the only Indians who have received recognition for their contributions to our armed forces are the "code talkers." These are the Native Americans from several tribes whose unique language skills were used to such good effect by the U.S. armed forces during World War I and II and Korea. The Indians could talk to each other using codes no one outside their tribes could understand. The Japanese so feared the code talkers that their soldiers were ordered to kill them instead of capturing them.

During the Vietnam War numerous non-Natives went to Canada to avoid military service because the draft was still in effect. However, I am proud to point out that many Canadian Indians came to the United States and enlisted in the U.S. Army and fought in Vietnam alongside American soldiers. I am sorry to say that these Native American volunteers from Canada have never been recognized for their contributions to the U.S. Army.

We Native Americans who have enlisted and served this country are extremely proud of our service, our sacrifices, and our accomplishments in time of war. Some of us came back uninjured, some came back wounded in mind or body, and some did not make it back at all.

—*Carson Walks Over Ice*
Crow Nation
Montana

PREFACE

American Indians have served in our nation's armed forces beginning with the War for Independence from Great Britain. In fact, Indians have been members of our country's armed forces even though they were not to become U.S. citizens until after World War I—a fact that has been largely overlooked by Americans who have grown up on a diet of cowboy and Indian movies and Wild West literature. Moreover, Indian veterans are honored and admired in their home communities as much as, if not more than, veterans in other American communities. Visit almost any reservation and one is struck by the number of American flags and Veterans of Foreign Wars posts. Indians continue to be represented in the armed forces in numbers that belie their small percentage of the U.S. population.

All Indian people take special pride in their veterans. The women actively promote and participate in commemorative events, including traditional dances and parades. Not only are Indians intensely patriotic, but they are prouder still to wear the uniform and to openly celebrate those who wear it, because military service reinforces age-old traditions that unify the entire community.

One reason for their participation is the opportunity to continue their warrior tradition. As a Ute friend once joked, "We Indians are grateful that the United States became such a militaristic country because it has provided us with an acceptable way to continue our warrior ways."

There is no better evidence of this than the records of Indians in the Vietnam War. Although thousands of American boys went to Canada to escape the draft, few, if any, of them were Indians. In fact, there was an opposite movement of Canadian Indians who came into the U.S. to enlist in a fighting unit.

Where once being a warrior was considered a man's job, today it is a vocation open to Indian women as well, as evidenced by the tragic story of Pvt. 1st Class Lori Ann Piestewa, who died in Iraq in 2003. Half Hopi and half Hispanic, Lori has received national recognition as the first American Indian woman killed in combat. Wayne Taylor, the Hopi tribal chairman, says the most frequently asked question on the Hopi reservation was: "Why did Lori join the Army?" Many theories have been offered. Perhaps it was because of the family's military legacy—her father had served in Vietnam and her grandfather in World War II. Or it may have been her ROTC training in high school. "The question," he says, "should not be why did she join, but rather, why is it strange for her to?"

Despite the remarkable record of American Indian patriotism and military service, it has been largely overlooked and even ignored by our nation's leaders. President George W. Bush admitted as much when, on March 3, 2008, he awarded the Medal of Honor to Master Sgt. Woodrow Wilson Keeble for military valor during the Korean War more than 25 years after this death. "Some blamed the bureaucracy for a shameful blunder," Bush said. "Others suspected racism. Whatever the reason, the first Sioux Indian ever to receive the Medal of Honor died without knowing it."

In truth, few Indian heroes are known outside of their tribes. I became aware of this largely unknown story through my work at the Smithsonian Institution as director of the National Anthropological Archives, which is one of the largest and finest collections of American Indian documents, photographs, and art in the United States. Upon becoming director in 1972, I initiated a program to help train Indians as archivists, librarians, and historians. As a result, I befriended dozens of Indian men and women who shared my interest in collecting and preserving Native American oral history.

One of these friends was Wolfrobe Hunt, a member of Acoma Pueblo, living in Tulsa, Oklahoma. He asked me to record certain Acoma sacred songs and prayers because he believed he was the last person who knew them and he wanted them preserved. He was worried these songs would be lost forever because the young people at Acoma were too infatuated with the glitz and glamour of contemporary American society to embrace traditional values and beliefs. I am pleased to say that after holding those recordings for more than 20 years they are now in the Acoma archives.

During these recording sessions, Wolfrobe sang the Acoma scalp song. I was surprised that the Acoma had such a song because the Pueblo people are noted for their pacifist ways. True, Wolfrobe said, but when necessary, they could be fearless warriors, and they had taken many scalps in their day. When did the Acoma take their last scalp? I asked.

Wolfrobe thought a minute and then said, "For sure it was during the Second World War. I know my uncle took a German scalp. It was in the closing days of the war. He was a soldier in the U.S. Army and he had been wounded during a fight to capture a city. He was lying semiconscious in a gutter along a street when two German soldiers walked past him. One of the soldiers gave him a kick to make sure he was dead. The kick jolted him to full consciousness. When he realized what had happened, he was so angry that he rolled over and tossed a hand grenade at the two soldiers, killing them both. Then he crawled over and scalped the one he thought had kicked him.

"Taking a scalp," Wolfrobe informed me, "carried responsibilities with it. The spirit of the person who had been scalped will always be hovering around, so my uncle had to take proper care of it. He had to feed it cornmeal and say the proper prayers so the spirit of the scalp owner did not harm him."

After hearing this story, I began asking other Native American friends about their modern military experiences. One of those friends—who later adopted me as his brother—is Joseph Medicine Crow, Ph.D., the Crow tribal historian. He is descended from a long line of Crow war chiefs including his grandfathers Medicine Crow and White Man Runs Him, who both aided the U.S. Army during the Indian wars.

Joseph, who was born in 1913, was in fact raised by pre-reservation Indians "still living in the past, still cherishing their traditional religion, philosophy, and way of life. For that reason," he says, "all the boys of my age on the Crow Reservation were brought up in two ways at the same time—to be warriors but also to succeed in the white man's world." That warrior training was put to good use during World War II when Private Medicine Crow earned a chieftainship from the Crow tribe for his battlefield exploits. For these exploits he also earned—from the white man's world—a Bronze Star and the French Legion of Honor Medal.

Another Crow friend, Mardel Plain Feather, introduced me to Carson Walks Over Ice, the recipient of a Purple Heart, a Bronze Star, and a Silver Star for his heroics in Vietnam. When I mentioned to her my interest in meeting native veterans for a possible book about Indians in the military, she said, "Well, then you will want to talk to my nephew, Carson Walks Over Ice. He is a decorated veteran of the Vietnam War, and his safe return was predicted in the Sun Dance. Everyone on the reservation knows that story." After reading this book, you will also know it.

Thanks to these friendships, I discovered that an important part of American history had not been recorded or documented. *Warriors in Uniform* is the result of that discovery, and my hope is that it will encourage other Native Americans to record and share their stories for the enlightenment and education of future generations of Americans, Indians, and non-Indians alike.

Herman J. Viola
Curator Emeritus
Smithsonian Institution

DEDICATION

THE WARRIOR SPIRIT

I close my eyes and all the noise around me fades . . .

I close my eyes and I am transported to another place . . .
home. The grass is lush green and the summer
breeze blows lightly on my face and the
smell of pine trees and happiness fill my nose . . .

I close my eyes and I can hear the drum beat in perfect
rhythm with my heart. The shrill cries of the
singers rise into the air and with every beat
my chest fills up with pride . . .

I close my eyes and I can see the warriors of my people
dance before me in such a way as to say, "We are
still here and we are strong . . ."

I close my eyes and I hear the voices of my ancestors
calling to me saying, "They could not put us down.
Despite every attempt they have made against us you stand
today . . . a YOUNG, STRONG, ANISHINABEKWE. Show
them the strength of the seventh fire. Your spirit is the
spirit of a million warriors, and no person or obstacle shall
put you down. We will always watch over you."

I close my eyes and grow stronger, even
for just a moment.

I close my eyes and I know . . . because I have the
strength of a nation beside me.

Alisha Schulman, Ojibwe
U.S. Military Academy, West Point
Class of 2009

THIS 1833 LITHOGRAPH SHOWS THE DEATH OF TECUMSEH AT THE BATTLE OF THE THAMES IN OCTOBER 1813.

Chapter One
BETWEEN TWO FIRES

JOSEPH BRANT, CHIEF OF THE
MOHAWK, WAS ALSO A BRITISH
MILITARY OFFICER DURING THE
AMERICAN REVOLUTION.

Thayeadanegea,
Joseph Brant
The Mohawk Chief.

Until the issue was finally resolved by the Civil War, America's Native peoples frequently found themselves caught between "two fires" of opposing military powers. During the American Revolution Indian loyalty was pulled between England and the colonies. During the War of 1812, their choice was between England and the United States. In the Civil War, it was between North and South. Nonetheless, much as the tribes would have preferred to remain neutral in these conflicts, they were drawn into the fray, and for the most part these conflicts became their own civil wars, splitting tribes as well as families. As a result, Indians have fought in every war our country has fought.

THE AMERICAN REVOLUTION

The die was first cast during the American War for Independence. Both sides initially sought neutrality from Indian tribes. It was not concern for Indian welfare that prompted this attitude, but awareness that they did not fight according to the rules of "civilized" warfare. Neither side wished to tarnish its image in the parlors of Europe by being the first to enlist "savages" in its armies.

Such scruples soon gave way to the necessities of this hard-fought conflict, with most tribes remaining loyal to the crown. The Indian choice was simple and pragmatic: Most of their trade goods came from England, whereas most trespassers on their hunting grounds were colonists. The fact that the Continental Congress offered the Delaware Indians their own state after the Revolution in return for their support indicates the desperation of the colonial cause. This offer, which the Delaware rejected, resembled a clause in a treaty with the Cherokees allowing them to send a representative to Congress. Neither option was likely to be accepted by the American public.

The tribes that became most directly involved in the American Revolution were the members of the Iroquois Confederacy. Powerful and primarily pro-British, the confederacy occupied a strategic location along the Hudson River between New England and the middle colonies. Of the six tribes in the confederacy, the Seneca, Mohawk, Cayuga, and Onondaga sided with the British; only the Oneida and Tuscarora took up the patriot cause. George Washington, for one, recognized the need for Indian soldiers. They could "be made of excellent use as scouts and light troops," he informed the Continental Congress. Accordingly, the Congress in 1776 authorized him to enlist 2,000. Eventually, of the 250,000 men who served in Washington's army, about 5,500 were Indians.

A number of the Indians who rallied to the patriot cause were descendants of the so-called Praying Indians of New England, whose communities dated from the 17th century and the proselytizing activities of the Puritan missionary John Eliot. Now fully assimilated and intermarried with their white and black neighbors, they little resembled their Mahican, Wappinger, and other tribal ancestors in appearance or culture.

Of these Christian Indians, the residents of Stockbridge, Massachusetts, stand out. Known

Recalled One White Comrade,
the Oneida "Fought Like Bull Dogs."

as the Stockbridge Indians after their mission village located in the Berkshire Mountains of Massachusetts, the members of this Christian community were primarily Mahican, but the group included other Native peoples from across New England. The Stockbridge Indians not only used their influence to keep other tribes from supporting the British, but they also formed a company in the colonial army and fought in every major campaign in the eastern theater of the American Revolution from Bunker Hill to the Battle of Monmouth.

Their effectiveness as a fighting unit ended in August 1778 when the Stockbridge company encountered a unit of the Queen's Rangers, mounted dragoons, near White Plains, New York. Although they were heavily outnumbered, the Indians fought gallantly, but they were no match for the horsemen who ran them down, killing or disabling some 40 of the Mahican patriots and capturing 10. After the battle, local residents buried the slain Stockbridge soldiers, including their chief, in a site now known as Indian Field in Van Cortlandt Park in the Bronx, New York.

THE ONEIDA
The Oneida Indians also paid a steep price for their loyalty to

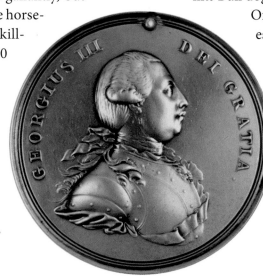

The George III friendship medal was distributed by the British to tribal leaders for loyalty and service.

the patriot cause. Like the Praying Indians, the Oneida were Christian, espousing the Presbyterian tenets of their beloved missionary Samuel Kirkland, a New England Puritan and ardent patriot. As early as 1775, the Oneida had organized their own militia company under Captain Tewahangaraghken, or Honyery Doxtator. According to his pension file in the National Archives, he organized a company of Oneida Indians "who were friendly to the Americans in their struggle for liberty, and entered the military service of the Revolutionary War."

At his side was his wife, Tyonajanegen, who, at the Battle of Oriskany Creek, not only handled her own musket but also loaded her husband's gun for him after a ball wounded his right wrist. Recalled one white comrade, the Oneida "fought like Bull dogs."

Oriskany was one of the bloodiest battles of the American Revolution. Hundreds of soldiers in the patriot ranks died that day. The battle also was a major factor in the breakup of the Iroquois Confederacy because it pitted some 60 Oneidas against an equal force of Mohawks and Senecas led by Mohawk leader Joseph Brant, who held a commission in the British Army.

As a result of Oneida support for the patriot cause, the

fui Indianer hu der Stockbridge Horde.

This 1778 depiction of a Stockbridge Indian shows that his weapons were both gun and arrows. The Stockbridge fought in every major campaign in the eastern theater of the American Revolution.

THIS PRINT DOCUMENTS FIGHTING DURING THE BATTLE OF ORISKANY CREEK, ONE OF THE BLOODIEST ENGAGEMENTS OF THE AMERICAN REVOLUTION.

One Oneida Fighting with the Americans Was Captured by His Own Brother.

American Revolution became a civil war for Iroquois as well as colonial families. One Oneida fighting with the Americans was captured by his own brother, a supporter of the British, who then turned him over to the Seneca for execution.

Although the Indians had little effect on the military outcome of the American Revolution, their participation produced two far-reaching emotional and psychological consequences that shaped white attitudes and U.S. government policy for decades. One was a reputation for brutality inspired by the atrocities that are inevitable in every war. The other was the notion that the Indians deserved punishment for siding with the British even though several tribes cast their lot with the colonies. To make matters worse for the Indians, no matter which side eastern tribes chose, the newly formed United States did not make any distinction.

THE WAR OF 1812

During the War of 1812, when the United States fought its second war of independence from England, tribal America again followed diverging courses. On the northern frontier, some Indians rallied to the vision of the Shawnee leader Tecumseh, who called for the tribes to unite against the United States. Tecumseh, a general in the British Army, died for his cause at the Battle of the Thames, during fighting in the Northwest.

In the South, the once powerful Creek Nation became so divided over allegiances between the United States and England that a civil war erupted between "Red Sticks" and "White Sticks." The breakup of tribal groups in the South presaged the sort of bitter fratricide that occurred during the Civil War as members of the so-called Five Civilized Tribes joined opposing forces.

Eventually, Andrew Jackson, with the aid of a Cherokee regiment and the support of the Choctaw led by Chief Pushmataha defeated the Red Sticks at the Battle of Horseshoe Bend in Alabama. Old Hickory then turned his attention to the British. Again drawing upon Indian allies, including 500 Choctaws, he attacked Pensacola, Florida. Later, at the Battle of New Orleans, Jackson's Choctaw allies led by Chief Pushmataha, buttressed his left flank.

Pushmataha, who died on Christmas Eve 1824, while on a visit to Washington, D.C., was rewarded for his loyalty to the United States with a state funeral. His dying wish—to "let the big guns be fired over me"—was honored by the Marine Corps under the direction of the secretary of the Navy and two companies of the District of Columbia militia. Two thousand congressmen, government officials, and citizens followed the cortege to Congressional Cemetery. The minute guns that thundered on Capitol Hill were echoed by three crisp musket volleys at graveside as the United States paid tribute to the Choctaw general.

THE SEMINOLE WARS

No such ceremony honored Maj. David Moniac, who was killed at the Battle of Wahoo Swamp in 1836 during the Second Seminole War. Moniac is considered by many to be the first Native American to graduate from the United States Military Academy at West Point.

Although a couple of other cadets could claim that distinction because of mixed ancestry, Moniac is the first cadet identified as such in surviving academy records.

Referred to as the Indian Boy by academy superintendent Sylvanus Thayer, the 15-year-old Creek youngster was admitted in 1817 under the terms of a 1790 treaty between the U.S. government and the Creek Nation. A secret codicil to that treaty provided that the U.S. government would bear the educational expenses for four Creek men, and the tribe selected Moniac to attend the academy. Even though Cadet Moniac spent an extra year at the academy in hopes

In this German portrait, Shawnee leader Tecumseh carries weapons of war. A general in the British Army during the War of 1812, Tecumseh died October 5, 1813, at the Battle of the Thames.

Among the American-made diplomatic gifts intended to win Indian friendship is this silver breastplate.

With the Second Seminole War going badly, the federal government promised to the Creek volunteers "the pay and emoluments and equipment of soldiers in the Army of the United States and such plunder as they may take from the Seminoles" for their service. Moniac was the only Indian among the 13 officers who commanded the regiment's 750 Creek volunteers. The Creeks, who wore white turbans to distinguish themselves from their kinsmen, earned their money. Their Seminole adversaries were virtually unbeatable in the swampy homeland they used to their advantage.

After leading an attack against a strong Seminole encampment near Tampa, Florida, in October 1836 Moniac was promoted to major, but his budding military career ended abruptly a month later. Part of a combined force consisting of the Creek Volunteers, Tennessee Volunteers, and Florida militia, Moniac pressed the attack against a group of Seminoles hiding in a cypress swamp behind a stream connecting two lakes. When the Creek dragoons hesitated, fearing the narrow stream was too deep to wade across, Moniac lifted his sword and plunged forward. The hidden Seminoles riddled him with numerous bullets. A witness to his death later wrote, "Major Moniac, an educated Creek warrior, in attempting to cross the creek, fell dead and the Seminoles were elated."

On Moniac's tombstone is engraved a quote by Gen. Thomas Sydney Jesup, commander of all U.S. troops in the Second Seminole War: "David Moniac was as brave as any man who has drawn a sword and faced the enemy." Perhaps a more appropriate epitaph—one that would serve for most warriors in uniform—was written by historian Kenneth L. Benton: "He died as he lived, in two worlds: as a Major in the service of the

of improving his class standing, he ranked only 39th out of 40 when he graduated on July 1, 1822. Then, after serving only about six months as a brevet second lieutenant in the Sixth Infantry Regiment, Moniac resigned his commission because of family problems back home. His decision was probably also eased somewhat by the suggestion of President James Madison that excess officers retire to civilian life, where they could impart the benefits of their West Point training to their state militias. Moniac did enlist in the Alabama state militia as a private, but he had more success as a farmer raising cotton and breeding horses.

Ironically, even though he was married to a cousin of the Seminole leader Osceola, Moniac agreed to join the fight against his Seminole kinsmen and in August 1836 was commissioned as a captain in the Mounted Creek Volunteers.

WARRIORS IN UNIFORM

United States Army—and as an Indian warrior in the service of his people."

THE CIVIL WAR

Another prominent Indian soldier in this period was Ely S. Parker, a New York Seneca chief who fought for the North during the Civil War. Parker became Gen. Ulysses S. Grant's secretary and achieved the rank of brigadier general. After the war, he became the first Native American to head the Bureau of Indian Affairs, the government agency that has controlled the destiny of the nation's Native peoples since its establishment in 1824.

Parker was educated at a Baptist mission school and later studied law, but he was denied admittance to the New York Bar because, as an Indian, he was not an American citizen. He then studied civil engineering at Rensselaer Polytechnic Institute. When the Civil War broke out, Parker offered his services as an army engineer but was refused a commission by both the governor of New York and Secretary of War Edwin Stanton, again because of his Indian heritage. The Civil War, Stanton explained to Parker, was a personal affair between white men, and he would do well to return home and tend his farm. Parker ignored this patronizing advice and continued to press for a commission, becoming a captain of engineers in 1863. Because of an earlier friendship with General Grant, he was assigned to his staff.

This lithograph depicts South Carolina soldiers along the Withlacoochee River during the Second Seminole War, which lasted from 1835 to 1842.

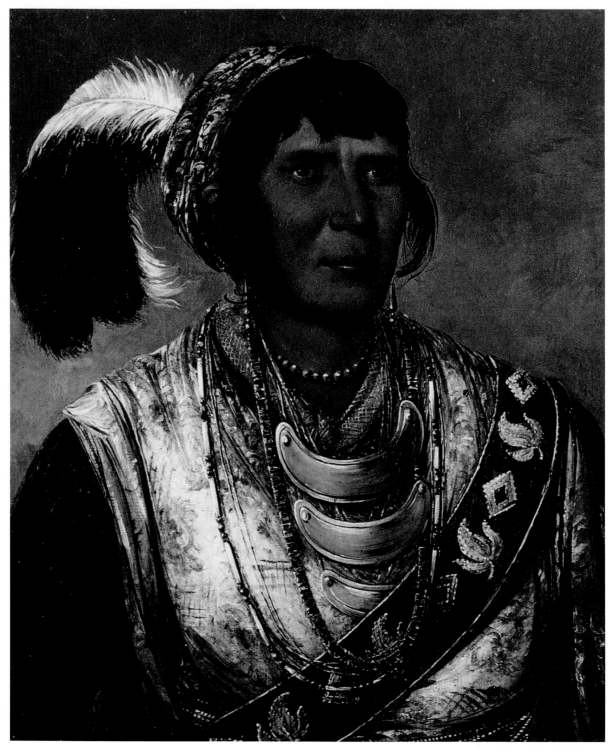

Osceola, one of the militant leaders in the Second Seminole War, was captured in violation of a truce and died in prison only a few days after George Catlin painted this striking portrait in 1837.

Gen. Ulysses S. Grant is shown with Ely S. Parker (seated at right), a Seneca who became Grant's secretary and achieved the rank of brigadier general during the Civil War.

As in the previous North American conflicts, the combatants welcomed Indians into their armies. Indeed, American Indians fought fiercely for both sides in the war. As historian Laurence Hauptman points out in his important study *Between Two Fires,* many fought because they believed it was their last best hope to halt the genocide that had begun on the East Coast, continued through the Trail of Tears westward through the 1830s, and then exploded after the gold rush of 1849. But, as Hauptman points out, "the Civil War, rather than the last best hope, proved to be the final nail in the coffin in Indian efforts to stop the tide of American expansion."

As many as 20,000 Indians served in Union and Confederate forces both on land and on sea. They were present at most of the major battles and participated in the heaviest fighting of the war, including Second Bull Run, Antietam, the Wilderness, Spotsylvania, Cold Harbor, and the Union assaults on Petersburg. It was Parker, Grant's secretary, who drew up the articles of Robert E. Lee's surrender at Appomattox, while the last Confederate general to lay down his arms—two months after Lee—was Stand Watie, the Cherokee commander of the Indian regiments fighting in the western theater.

CONFEDERATE SOLDIERS

For the Confederacy, Indian manpower was especially important, and southern agents actively sought Native American allies, especially among the Five Civilized Tribes—the Cherokee, Chickasaw, Choctaw, Creek, and Seminole—all of them former slaveholding peoples, despite the fact that slaveholding practices and attitudes among them

WARRIORS IN UNIFORM

Native warriors began wearing military uniforms during the colonial wars of empire when the European powers launched the contest for control of North America. Native friendship and manpower were especially important in these conflicts. As a result, these countries went to great lengths to gain Native loyalty and military support.

An essential component of their diplomatic efforts was the presentation of gifts of state that conveyed power and authority to the recipients. These gifts included flags, silver medals, uniforms, and weapons such as swords, tomahawks, and guns. The weapons often were engraved and even

Charles Bird King painted this portrait of Choctaw chief Pushmataha during the chief's visit to Washington, D.C., in 1824. The chief died soon after and was buried in Congressional Cemetery.

personalized, like the tomahawk shown here that was presented to Tecumseh, the Shawnee leader, by his British patrons during the War of 1812. The inscription reads, "To Chief Tecumseh from Col Proctor MDCCCXII."

On this page, at left, is the portrait of the Choctaw chief Pushmataha painted by Charles Bird King. Shown here in full military uniform, Pushmataha was a commissioned officer in the U.S. Army. He earned his epaulets during the War of 1812, when he raised a force of 500 Choctaw soldiers who served with distinction in various engagements, including the Battle of New Orleans.

Pushmataha had demonstrated his loyalty to the American cause before the war, in a dramatic confrontation with Tecumseh, who visited Choctaw country hoping to gain the tribe's support for his pan-Indian alliance against the U.S.: "Tecumseh," he said, "you have made your choice. You have elected to fight with the British. The Americans have been our friends and we shall stand by them. If, after this decision, any Choctaw should be so foolish as to follow your imprudent advice and enlist to fight against the Americans, thereby abandoning his own people . . . Pushmataha will see that proper punishment is meted out to him, which is death."

Popularly known as the Indian General, he was a strict disciplinarian who was well liked by his fellow officers; they accorded him the status that befitted his rank on all public, social, and official occasions. When he died during a visit to Washington, D.C., in December 1824, he was buried with full military honors. John Randolph of Roanoke, who eulogized him on the Senate floor, characterized Pushmataha as "one of nature's nobility, a man who would have adorned any society."

THIS TOMAHAWK WAS PRESENTED TO THE SHAWNEE LEADER TECUMSEH, WHO FOUGHT ON BEHALF OF THE BRITISH DURING THE WAR OF 1812.

Union Army Commanders Regarded Indians as an Enemy to Be Fought.

varied. That these tribes joined the Confederacy was perhaps inevitable because the land they occupied adjoined Confederate states and many of their mixed-blood leaders were slaveholders sympathetic to the southern cause.

Moreover, the Confederate states offered them equal status in the Confederate government. The tribes could send representatives to the Confederate Congress and had the right to tax merchants and traders within their boundaries. The Confederate government also promised the tribes compensation for damages caused by intruders during the war.

FOR THE UNION

As a result of Confederate inducements, the five tribes formally joined the Confederacy and more than 15,000 uniformed Indian soldiers fought for the southern cause, primarily in the western theater, with Pea Ridge in Arkansas their most significant battle.

Perhaps as many as 4,000 Indians fought for the North. Some served in the infantry; others were scouts and sharpshooters. The Indian volunteers wore their uniforms as proudly as their white comrades-in-arms did, and they suffered the same horrendous casualty rates as their white compatriots in this unbelievably brutal and bloody war. For example, of the 135 Oneida volunteers from Wisconsin in the Union Army, only 55 returned home, a mortality rate of nearly 41 percent.

Parker and a few other Indians received commissions in the Union Army and were recognized for their contributions to the war effort,

but such cases were rare. If the truth be told, Union Army commanders regarded Indians as an enemy to be fought, not as warriors to be welcomed in their ranks. Had it not been for the early recruitment of Indians by the Confederacy, it is unlikely that the Union Army would have enlisted any Indians at all. Indeed, as early as July 1861, Brig. Gen. Albert Pike had succeeded in raising a regiment of Creek tribal members in the Indian Territory for Confederate service. By November the South had filled four complete Indian regiments.

On the Union side, the War Department, as well as the professional officer corps in general, opposed the recruitment of Indian troops. Besides uncertainty about the reliability of Indian soldiers, there was concern that they would not fight according to the rules and standards taught at West Point. As one Union officer reportedly said, "It is not the policy of our government to fight high-toned southern gentlemen with Indians." The officer corps also believed that the Indians' lack of discipline and training would make them ineffectual soldiers.

Nonetheless, in the spring of 1862 the secretary of the interior formally requested that President Lincoln authorize several Indian regiments to be recruited from refugees driven from Indian Territory by their pro-Confederate brethren.

Although Lincoln and his Cabinet concluded that neither Indian nor Negro units could be enlisted under the provision authorizing the enlistment of volunteer troops, they did agree to create a "Home Guard" of loyal Indians for local service. The secretary of war was then directed

A group of Cherokee Confederate veterans gather for a reunion in 1901 in North Carolina. Chickasaw, Choctaw, Creek, and Seminole also sided with the Confederacy during the Civil War.

to enlist two or more Indian regiments in the Department of the Missouri. Although the Indians were to be a Home Guard, their obvious objective would be the recovery of lost homes and lands, and therefore it would be a case of Indians fighting Indians.

The formation of the Home Guard regiments almost did not occur, because the local Union commander simply forbade it. In fact, he threatened to arrest any officer who recruited Indians. At this strategic moment the former Department of Kansas was reestablished, and the new commander ordered that the Indian regiments be formed as quickly as possible.

The first military expedition—consisting of two Creek and Cherokee regiments, five white regiments, and two artillery batteries—was launched soon afterward. This expedition set the pattern of subsequent Indian participation in the war, which consisted of a series of expeditions into Indian Territory to restore the refugee Indians to their homes, neutralize the Confederate Indian force, and establish a base of operations from which to strike at Confederate forces in the West. The Indians performed so well that the War Department not only relaxed its objections to their use but looked into making them eligible for the draft as the manpower demands

DELAWARE INDIANS REST AFTER A RECONNAISSANCE MISSION ON BEHALF OF THE UNION ARMY DURING THE CIVIL WAR.

The Indian Soldier Had Little Time to Learn the White Man's Military Methods and Codes.

of the Civil War mushroomed. The inquiry got no further than the Department of the Interior, which pointed out that Indians were not citizens and thus could not be drafted.

OPPOSITION

The original objections of Union officers to Indian soldiers appeared well founded after the Battle of Pea Ridge, Arkansas, in March 1862, when some of the Union dead had obviously been scalped. Further evidence of scalping was found among both the Confederate and Union dead the following September, after the Battle of Newtonia, Missouri. This was one of the few battles of the Civil War in which significant numbers of Indians fought on both sides. These discoveries concerned both Union and Confederate commanders, who thereafter refrained from making use of Indian soldiers outside of Indian Territory.

Of more concern, however, was the lack of discipline and military deportment of the Indian soldiers, but what could the professional officer corps expect? Hastily recruited and put into battle, the Indian soldier had little time to learn the white man's military methods and codes, even had he been so inclined. Accustomed to individual, guerrilla-type warfare, the Indian soldiers preferred to fight from behind trees and rocks. Also disconcerting to white commanders was the Indian soldier's general ignorance of English, which made it difficult to execute oral or written commands, his disdain for routine camp duties, and his lack of concern about the proper cleanliness and care of his uni-

form. Most distressing was the Indian soldier's inclination to wander off on occasion. Regulations about unauthorized absences, one of the cornerstones of military discipline, meant little to Indian soldiers who often came and went as they pleased. Desertion was also common since the Indian soldiers usually had no loyalties to the cause other than reclaiming or protecting their homes and lands. When, for example, the first Home Guard expedition into Indian Territory captured the Cherokee capital of Tahlequah, an entire regiment of Confederate Indians deserted to the Union side.

Regardless of what some officers may have thought about warriors in uniform, General Grant obviously valued the services of Ely Parker. When Grant needed someone to draft a congratulatory letter to his army after its victory at Chattanooga, he gave the task to Parker because "he was good at that sort of thing." At Appomattox Court House, Grant assigned him the task of transcribing the articles of surrender because, as one of the Union officers admitted, Parker's handwriting was so much better than anyone else's.

Robert E. Lee at first seemed taken aback by the dark-skinned Parker, when Grant introduced the Confederate general to his staff. Perhaps he thought that Grant was making a point by having a black soldier present at the surrender ceremony before realizing that Parker was a Native American. While shaking Parker's hand Lee said, "I am glad to see one real American here." To which Parker replied, "Sir, we are all Americans."

Thomas Bigford of Taycheeda, Wisconsin, a recruiter and farmer, swears in two Native American soldiers to fight with the Union Army during the Civil War.

SYMBOLS OF NATIONALISM

The most important diplomatic gifts given to Indian leaders were medals and flags. These carried the full weight of national allegiance and conferred upon the recipients added status and rank within their tribes. All the colonial powers, including Russia, gave such gifts. Indeed, by 1789 the custom had become so fixed that the newly established United States had no choice but to continue the practice. Thus, beginning with the administration of George Washington, the young nation continued to give tribal leaders diplomatic gifts to gain their friendship and loyalty. Known as peace medals because many bore symbols of friendship such as clasped hands on the obverse, the American medals were solid silver and featured the likeness of the incumbent President. With the exception of John Adams, each President from George Washington to Benjamin Harrison issued peace medals to Indian leaders. Shown here is Charles Bird King's portrait of Seneca chief Red Jacket. Red Jacket proudly wears the friendship medal he received from George Washington. The medal, which appears on the opposite page, is in the custody of the Buffalo and Erie County Historical Society.

A Charles Bird King portrait shows Seneca chief Red Jacket wearing his George Washington peace medal.

THOMAS JEFFERSON PEACE MEDAL
The first minted medal, it bears the clasped hands of friendship, a symbol on all the presidential medals until the Zachary Taylor Administration.

GEORGE WASHINGTON MEDAL
This peace medal was given to Seneca chief Red Jacket by President George Washington, in Philadelphia, in 1792.

RUSSIAN FRIENDSHIP MEDAL
This medal was given to Indian leaders by Russian emissaries. The inscription reads "Allies of Russia."

A GROUP OF APACHE SCOUTS POSE
WITH THEIR INTERPRETER (FAR LEFT)
AND COMMANDING OFFICER (FAR
RIGHT) IN ARIZONA IN 1882.

Chapter Two

THE U.S. ARMY:
AGENT OF ASSIMILATION

OGLALA LAKOTA WARRIOR NO
FLESH POSES IN FULL UNIFORM
FOR A STUDIO ALBUMEN
PORTRAIT TAKEN CA 1890.

When the guns of the Civil War at last fell silent, the U.S. Army underwent a dramatic drop in manpower. Authorized strength fell from 57,000 in 1867 to half that a decade later and then averaged 26,000 until the war with Spain at century's end. Effective strength, however, always fell short of authorized strength because of high rates of sickness and desertion, so the Army was hard-pressed to provide the command and control necessary to maintain order and safety across the Far West.

Although this was an era of international peace for the United States, on the domestic front it was far different. The years following the Civil War witnessed a dramatic increase in violence across the West as various Indian tribes lashed out at the tide of white settlement that poured across the Mississippi River after Appomattox.

AN INVALUABLE ALLY

Faced with the realities of a shrinking army and a huge territory to patrol and pacify, military forces in the West, both professional and volunteer, increasingly came to make use of friendly Indians in their conflicts with the hostiles. Some of the arrangements with these Indian allies were informal, with captured horses, weapons, and other booty being the only payment necessary for their services. In other situations, however, the Indians were enlisted into formally organized and officered militia units just as had been the case with volunteer troops by Confederate and Union forces during the Civil War. As a result, the concept of the Indian as the enemy slowly gave way to the reality that in western warfare the Indian could be an invaluable ally against other Indians.

Recognizing this, Congress in 1866 authorized the Army to enlist up to 1,000 Indians "to act as scouts . . . [and to] receive the pay and allowances of cavalry soldiers." Although seldom more than a third that number were in the ranks over the next three decades, the door had been opened to permit American Indians to serve as enlisted personnel in the U.S. Army. The scouts served six-month tours of duty with the option to reenlist if they wished. Many did so, forming a core group of enlistees who played important roles in campaigns against hostile Indians across the West until the era of the Indian wars drew to a close at the end of the 19th century.

For many of the Indians who served as Army scouts and auxiliaries, this was their introduction to white culture, their first significant exposure to white ways of thinking and doing things. In fact, some of the professional officer corps viewed the use of Indians in this manner as a useful step in the process of assimilating these tribesmen into mainstream society.

One of the officers who believed this was John J. Pershing, who was stationed on the Pine Ridge Indian Reservation in South Dakota in the early 1890s upon graduating from West Point.

Later, in his autobiography, Pershing extolled the virtues of his Indian soldiers. They readily learned English, and they provided a good example to other Indians. "It would have been an excellent idea," he declared, "to have formed one or two permanent regiments of . . . [Indians] as we had with the Negroes. Nothing would have done more to teach them loyalty to the government nor have gone further to bring them to civilized ways."

Because of his favorable experience with his warriors in uniform, Pershing—almost alone among the professional officer corps—supported the concept of separate Native units in World War I.

Church groups, humanitarians, and other reformers, however, did not share Pershing's optimism. They believed that encouraging the warrior way of life did the Indians a disservice. Indians should be encouraged to become farmers, not fighters, insisted the reformers and other white benefactors, who saw the warrior

mind-set as the root cause of the "savagery" from which they hoped to rescue the Indians.

Nonetheless, when given the option, most western tribesmen welcomed the opportunity to join the Army as scouts and auxiliaries just so they could continue their warrior way of life as long as possible. Who could blame them? "A reservation is a prison," declared James Kaywaykla. As a child he had been one of the band members under Mimbres Apache raider Victorio. "Ours was a race of fighting men—war was our occupation," he boasted. "A rifle was our most cherished possession . . . there was not a man [on the reservation] who did not envy the scout with his rifle."

Little wonder, then, that men who regarded warfare as honorable and horses and weapons as the tools of manhood should find Army service attractive. And, as soldiers, their adjustment to

U.S. Cavalry Company B, made up of Lakota, poses with its commander, Lt. John J. Pershing, on the Pine Ridge Reservation in South Dakota in 1891.

WARRIORS IN UNIFORM

"Ours Was a Race of Fighting Men— War Was Our Occupation."

the white way of life was less drastic, enabling them to meet their inevitable future somewhat on their own terms. Several tribes—notably the Tonkawa, the Warm Springs of Oregon, the Pawnee, the Wyoming Shoshone, and the Crow—maintained long-term relationships with the Army.

A COMMON ENEMY

For the Crow Nation that relationship was dictated by the harsh realities of life on the northern plains after the Civil War as various tribes fought with each other as well as with white settlers over an ever shrinking land base. The Crow, whose traditional homeland encompassed a vast area that stretched across much of present-day Wyoming and Montana, were surrounded by several numerically superior and militant tribes including the Sioux, the Cheyenne, and the Blackfoot. Constant warfare with these traditional enemies made the Crow a brave and hardy people. It also helped explain why they allied themselves with the U.S. Army: Its enemies—the Sioux and Cheyenne—were also their enemies.

The violence on the northern plains escalated when the federal government opened a route in 1864 linking the Oregon Trail to the gold fields of Montana. Known as the Bozeman Trail, the road passed through pristine hunting grounds that belonged to the Crow but that were also coveted by the Sioux and Cheyenne, who immediately attacked any white travelers they encountered. To protect travelers, the U.S. Army built a string of three forts along the trail—Phil Kearny, C. F. Smith, and Reno.

The posts had minimal garrisons and no Indian scouts, although 50 had been authorized. The Crow offered to provide 250 warriors to help protect the forts, but Cdr. C. F. Carrington turned them down. He claimed he lacked both the authority to enlist them and the weapons needed to equip them. As a result, the posts endured months of siege conditions orchestrated by Red Cloud, the brilliant Oglala leader.

Fort Phil Kearny, Carrington's headquarters, sustained more Indian attacks than any other post in American history, culminating in the destruction on December 21, 1866, of more than half his garrison in the Fetterman Fight. Crow Indian scouts doubtless would have alerted the garrison to the massive ambush that awaited Capt. William J. Fetterman and his 80 troopers.

Although never given any official status, the Crow remained in the area of the Bozeman Trail outposts until the Army abandoned them in 1868. Had it not been for their presence, Fort C. F. Smith, which was even more isolated than Fort Phil Kearny, might have fared just as badly, but it was more centrally located in Crow country, and the Sioux and Cheyenne had no desire to tangle with the Crow.

In truth, the local military commanders did not trust the Crow and therefore took little stock of their advice and warnings. Typical of the attitudes of the professional soldiers at these posts is a series of newspaper articles by Lt. George Palmer, who was stationed at Fort C. F. Smith. Shortly after his arrival, Palmer wrote, "There is not one redeeming trait about the character of any Indian, living or dead." A few months later

WARRIORS IN UNIFORM

IN AN 1876 ENGRAVING, SIOUX
AND CHEYENNE WARRIORS
CHARGE TROOPS LED BY
GEN. GEORGE CROOK AT THE
BATTLE OF THE ROSEBUD.

"No Other Indians Are Braver or Better Fighters Than the Crows."

he conceded that Indian troubles were sometimes the fault of corrupt government officials. Later—after befriending some Crows, spending time with them, and sharing a meal in their lodges—he gave grudging admiration to their warrior qualities, declaring that "no other Indians are braver or better fighters than the Crows." By then, the change in attitude was too late to save the posts, which Red Cloud burned after the Army vacated them.

Medicine Crow led a force of warriors fighting for Gen. George Crook as allies, not scouts.

LESSONS LEARNED

Having learned a bitter lesson along the Bozeman Trail, the Army ten years later made ample use of Indian auxiliaries in the campaign to force Sitting Bull, Crazy Horse, and their defiant followers onto the Great Sioux Reservation.

In the spring of 1876, the Army sent three columns of troops to converge upon and trap the last free-roaming Indians, who were thought to be somewhere in the Bighorn Country. One column, under Gen. George Crook, marched northward from Fort Fetterman on the Upper North Platte River. A second column, headed by Col. John Gibbon, moved eastward from Fort Ellis in Montana. A third column, led by Gen. Alfred Terry with the Seventh Cavalry, commanded by Lt. Col. George Armstrong Custer, ventured west from Fort Lincoln in the Dakota Territory.

Crook, a major proponent of employing Indian allies to fight Indians—and who later successfully employed Apache soldiers to fight hostile Apaches—dispatched emissaries to the Crow Agency near Livingston, Montana, requesting the aid of Crow warriors in the campaign against the Sioux and Cheyenne. The Crow authorized a force of 176 warriors led by Chiefs Medicine Crow and Plenty Coups to join Crook—but as fighting allies and not merely as noncombatant scouts. With Crook were also a number of Shoshone under the leadership of Chief Washakie.

Thanks to his Indian auxiliaries Crook was saved from the fate that befell Custer a few days later. A large force of Sioux and Cheyenne led by Crazy Horse almost caught the troopers by

Participants in the Battle of the Little Bighorn, including White Man Runs Him (second from left), pose in 1926 on the 50th anniversary of the battle at a monument to those who fought.

surprise as they prepared breakfast along the banks of the Rosebud River. The subsequent Battle of the Rosebud, fought June 17, 1876, saw fighting between the Lakota and Cheyenne and the Crow and Shoshone.

According to the Indian combatants, the soldiers were just there, and sometimes they were in the way. Although there were few casualties on either side, Crook's troopers expended so much ammunition in the six-hour fight that he retreated after Crazy Horse's followers returned to their camp along the Little Bighorn River.

LITTLE BIGHORN
Unaware of Crook's defeat, Terry and Gibbon met at the junction of the Rosebud and Yellow-

stone Rivers without encountering any Indians. Upon receiving word that scouts had spotted a fresh trail heading toward the Little Bighorn, Terry sent Custer and the Seventh Cavalry south along the Rosebud in hopes of finding Sitting Bull's camp. Once he found it, Custer was to block the Indian retreat into the Bighorn Mountains and await reinforcements.

With Custer were 47 Indian scouts—a few dozen Arikara, four Sioux married to Arikara women, and six Crows. One of the Crow scouts was White Man Runs Him, whose grandson Joseph Medicine Crow (see Chapter 4) was to earn his war honors as an infantryman fighting the Germans in World War II. Custer admired his Crow scouts, describing them in a letter to

"Custer's Last Rally," a monumental oil on canvas by John Mulvany completed in 1881, captures the romantic image that prevailed of the 1876 battle between followers of Sitting Bull and the Seventh Cavalry.

his wife, Libby, as "magnificent looking men, so much handsomer and more Indian-like than any we have ever seen, and so jolly and sportive; nothing of the gloomy, silent Redman about them." Indians had heard that Custer was tough, that he never abandoned a trail, and that when his food ran out he would eat mule. "That was the kind of man they wanted to fight under; they were willing to eat mule, too."

Custer may have admired his Crow scouts, but he failed to heed their advice. As White Man Runs Him later told his grandson, the Crow scouts succeeded in finding Sitting Bull's camp, but they also warned Custer that the

WARRIORS IN UNIFORM

enemy force was too large for the Seventh Cavalry to handle and advised him to await the promised reinforcements. Custer refused, lest Sitting Bull escape and deprive him of the victory he so desperately wanted and anticipated. Upon learning that Son of the Morning Star (the Crow name for Custer) planned an immediate attack, the scouts began removing their uniforms and putting on traditional fighting regalia. "What are they doing?" Custer asked Mitch Bouyer, his chief of scouts. When Bouyer repeated the question to the scouts, one of them pointed his finger at Custer and said in Crow: "Tell this man he's crazy! He is no good. Tell him that in a very short time we are all going to walk a path we never walked before. When we meet the Great Spirit, we want to be dressed as Crow warriors not as white men!" Custer, on

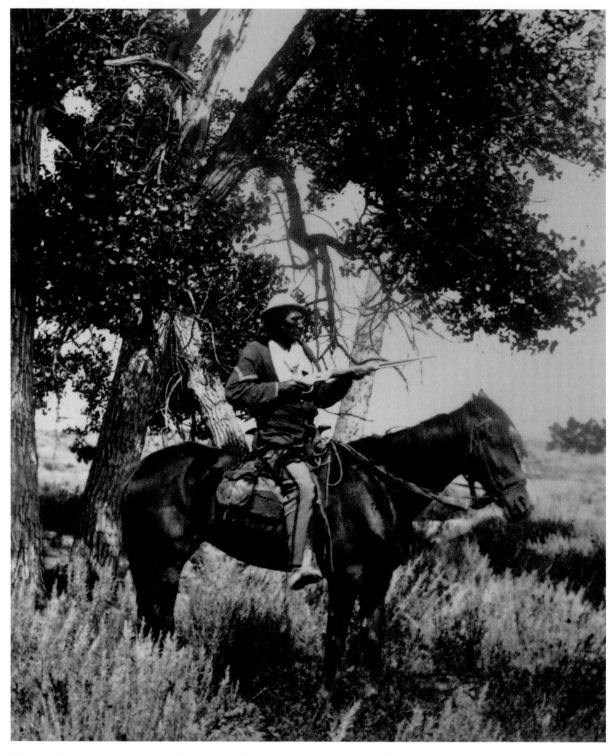

Custer's favorite scout, Bloody Knife, who was killed at the Battle of the Little Bighorn, is shown scouting during the Yellowstone Expedition of 1873.

WARRIORS IN UNIFORM

Chiricahua prisoners including Geronimo (first row, third from right) are photographed outside their railroad car in Arizona.

hearing this, ordered the Crow scouts to leave. "I don't want that defeatist attitude around my soldiers," he told Bouyer. "We'll do the fighting if they are so afraid of the Sioux." Thus none of the Crow scouts died that day, although three Arikara were killed, including Custer's favorite scout, Bloody Knife.

RESISTING CONFINEMENT

The decimation at the Little Bighorn could have been averted had Custer heeded the advice of his Crow scouts. There are examples of how Indians helped white soldiers avoid disaster, including one provided by Apache scouts who helped the Army against their hostile kinsmen. By the 1880s, of all the tribes that had once roamed freely over the American West, only a few Apache bands still resisted reservation life. Given the reservation allotted to them, Apache hostility is not difficult to understand. As part of an ongoing consolidation program, the Bureau of Indian Affairs assigned all the various Apache bands to San Carlos, a large reservation west of the Rio Grande along the Gila River. Of all the godforsaken pieces of landscape in which the federal government placed Indians, San Carlos was

Geronimo (left center), in a meeting with Gen. George Crook (far right), agreed to surrender two months after a raid on the Apache camp in the Sierra Madre. Two nights later he changed his mind and fled.

one of the worst. "There was nothing but cactus, rattlesnakes, heat, rocks, and insects," recalled one of the Apaches who lived there. "No game, no edible plants. Many, many of our people died of starvation."

Although most of the Apaches did their best to adjust to life there, two important and effective leaders refused. One was Victorio of the Mimbres, who took to the warpath when the government refused his requests to leave San Carlos. For a year his warriors raided unchecked across Texas, New Mexico, and northern Mexico, attacking isolated ranches and travelers with American and Mexican troopers constantly at his heels. The end came on October 15, 1880, when Tarahumara Indian scouts led Mexican soldiers to Victorio's hidden camp in the Chihuahua foothills known as Tres Castillos. Unable to escape, the Apaches fought desperately, at times fighting hand to hand. Of the 150 or so Apaches in the camp, 68 were captured, but 78 were killed—one of them Victorio.

The other Apache raider of note was Geronimo of the Chiricahua. Unhappy with reservation life, always ill-tempered, but also crafty and cunning, Geronimo decided to leave San Carlos in August 1881 following a disturbance caused by the Army's attempt to arrest a medicine man preaching a new and—according to white observers—inflammatory religion. With Geronimo went some hundred men, women, and children. A few months later he returned in dramatic fashion, killing the San Carlos police chief and forcing several hundred Chiricahuas to join him in Mexico.

WARRIORS IN UNIFORM

Crook . . . Enlisted Five Companies of Chiricahua Scouts—"The Wildest I Could Get," He Boasted.

The result was another Apache war that kept the Southwest in turmoil for the next five years. Wily, implacable, and tough, the Chiricahua were conquered only because the U.S. Army enlisted fellow tribesmen, conceding that only an Apache could catch an Apache. Credit for the tactic goes to Gen. George Crook, who had enjoyed considerable success fighting Apaches before his embarrassment at the Battle of the Rosebud against the Lakota and Cheyenne. Returned by the Army to the scene of his earlier success, Crook imposed military rule on San Carlos and enlisted five companies of Chiricahua scouts—"the wildest I could get," he boasted. They were tough as well as "wild": Eleven of the Medals of Honor given to Indian soldiers in the 19th century went to Apache scouts.

The Apache trademarks were stealth and surprise, easily achieved since war parties seldom numbered more than two dozen men. Typical was a raid in 1883 led by Chato, one of the more notorious Chiricahua freedom fighters. On March 21 Chato and some two dozen men crossed the border into Arizona, raided for six days, killed at least 11 people, covered more than 400 miles, lost only one man, and then slipped back into the Sierra Madre of Mexico without having been seen by any of the military units attempting to intercept him.

This time Crook and his Apache scouts took up the trail. Now, thanks to an agreement with Mexico that granted U.S. forces permission to cross the border when in hot pursuit of Apache raiders, the international boundary no longer provided protection to the fugitives. When the scouts surprised Chato in his high mountain hideout, a lair no outsider had ever before breached, the raiders knew the old way of life was over. One by one the band leaders, including Geronimo, met with Crook and surrendered.

Crook's success was short-lived. Geronimo soon tired of life at San Carlos, and in May 1885 he broke out again, taking more than a hundred people with him, including Naiche, the Apache chief Cochise's youngest son; Chihuahua, an Apache chief; and Nana, who was married to Geronimo's sister. Once again the scouts found them hidden in the Sierra Madre, and once again Geronimo met with General Crook and agreed to surrender, even though he was told they would have to be confined in the East for two years.

Crook hurriedly left to telegraph the good news to his superiors, while the prisoners followed at a leisurely pace toward the border. Along the way, the Apaches fell in with a whiskey peddler. The result was a change of heart on the part of Geronimo, who rushed back to the Sierra Madre with 20 men and 13 women.

This time Geronimo's behavior had disastrous consequences for his Chiricahua kinsmen. For letting him get away, Crook lost his command to Gen. Nelson Miles, who determined the strategy that finally brought the Apache wars to a conclusion. One reason the diehards had been so successful in maintaining their independence was their ability to visit relatives at San Carlos. These visits provided occasional reinforcements and opportunities for rest and resupply. Miles, therefore, deported all the Chiricahua Apaches,

Gen. Nelson Miles and his staff view the large Indian camp near Pine Ridge, South Dakota, a few days after the conflict that occurred at nearby Wounded Knee Creek on December 28, 1890.

including the scouts who had fought with the U.S. Army against their untamed kinsmen, to the Castillo de San Marcos in St. Augustine and other detention camps in Florida and Alabama. The deportation was as cruel as it was effective. The Chiricahuas were shipped by train to Florida in August 1886. Geronimo surrendered for the last time only a few weeks later.

Only once did the use of Indians to fight Indians backfire. In 1881 some Apache scouts turned on their fellow soldiers at Cibeque Creek in Arizona Territory. The mutiny resulted in the execution of three Apache scouts found guilty of murder and desertion in the face of the enemy.

Certainly some adjustments had to be made by officers who commanded the Indian scouts.

One was to accept the significance of the supernatural in their lives. To the Indians, it was a matter of the highest importance. To many white observers, it smacked of superstition. At best, it was a nuisance; at worst, it hindered military efficiency. Some officers did recognize the importance of religious ceremonials and protective "medicine" to the Indian warrior's morale. George Custer allowed his Arikara scouts to perform the proper ceremonies before going into action. Scout Red Star later said, "Custer had a heart like an Indian." George Crook, who commanded a large force of Apache scouts, once authorized them to hold a war dance so they could be assured of spiritual protection before setting out on one of his campaigns.

Troop L of the Third U.S. Cavalry, shown in front of their quarters, was composed of Indians, following an 1891 U.S. Army directive.

SOLDIERS, NOT SCOUTS

The culmination of the assimilation program came at the end of the Indian wars, perhaps as a means of continuing Army control over Indians when the need for it was fading away. Following the Wounded Knee Massacre in December 1890, the Army experimented with enlisting Indians not as short-term scouts but as soldiers serving five-year tours of duty in regular units. A directive issued in 1891 authorized changing the composition of Troop L in selected U.S. Cavalry regiments and Company I in selected U.S. Infantry regiments to 55 Indian enlisted personnel for each troop. The white enlisted men in these companies were either transferred or discharged and the vacancies were filled with Indians, usually from the same tribe. The idea was

to help the Indians assimilate into mainstream American society while earning an income. The initial recruitment was to be 1,000 men; they counted against the authorized ceiling of 25,000 active-duty personnel in the peacetime Army.

The program at first enjoyed remarkable success. The new recruits excelled in all facets of military deportment. An Apache company organized at Mount Vernon Barracks in Alabama from former prisoners of war proved so efficient at drill that the regimental commander placed it in a position of honor in battalion demonstrations. The Apache soldiers relished every opportunity to wear dress uniforms and demonstrate their abilities on the parade ground. Their commanding officer judged their intelligence to be far superior to that of the local citizens,

One Writer Said the Indian "Doesn't Have the Patriotic Instincts a Soldier Must Have."

especially the "sand hill tackies" who hovered around the base ridiculing the Apache soldiers.

Despite the evident success of the program, however, some officers expressed concern about employing Indians as soldiers. Indians admittedly did well on frontier duty fighting other Indians, the critics conceded, but could they perform as well quelling domestic disturbances such as labor strikes and racial disorders in urban settings? Why risk jeopardizing Army effectiveness, the critics also asked, simply to provide employment to a small percentage of America's disadvantaged population? Indeed, some said, why should "dangerous savages" receive such favored treatment? One writer to the *Army and Navy Journal* (May 16, 1891) reminded its readers that Greece, Carthage, and Rome had fallen, in part, because of their reliance on barbaric mercenaries. He predicted that the use of Indian soldiers would eventually undermine the moral fiber of America, declaring that the Indian simply "doesn't have the patriotic instincts a soldier must have."

The critics never had to confront their worst fears because the experiment fell apart of its own accord. After the initial success, recruitment among reservation Indians faltered badly. Despite extensive efforts to attract recruits from eastern Indian schools, by the summer of 1895, the original 1,000 Indian soldiers had dwindled to 67 men at Fort Sill, Oklahoma. This was Troop L of the Seventh Cavalry commanded by Capt. Hugh Scott. Most of the other Indian companies had only their white cadres. The units stayed on active duty another two years, when the adjutant general reported there had been no enlistments

or reenlistments in any of the units. On May 31, 1897, the Army declared the experiment a failure and discharged Scott's Troop L.

Why did the experiment fail? It was not the discipline or drill the Indian soldiers disliked; they could handle whatever the Army handed them. Rather, they objected to a system that violated cultural values such as making them cut their hair and live in framed buildings. They did not like the long-term enlistments or being stationed far away from their families. They also disliked much of the manual labor, which they called "women's work." On the part of the Army, the core of the problem may have been latent racism. Gen. O. O. Howard, the famed Civil War officer and founder of Howard University, the black college in Washington, D.C., said the experiment had been doomed from its inception because of the fear that one day white soldiers would have to take orders from Indian noncommissioned officers. Twenty years after his troop of Indian soldiers had been discharged, Hugh Scott, now a general in the U.S. Army, confided to a friend that the Indian soldiers had been cheated of their success by an air of prejudice in the War Department.

A POSITIVE RESULT

Nonetheless, the experiment with all-Indian units did have positive results if integration into white society was the desired outcome. Legislation passed in 1894 prohibited aliens who could not speak, read, or write English from enlistment in the U.S. Army. The law, a reflection of the nativism of the time, was

Sgt. W. J. McClure, a Choctaw, was a veteran of the 1898 Philippine campaign.

During the Spanish-American War, some effort was made to organize all-Indian units, but none succeeded. William F. Cody, better known as Buffalo Bill, offered to organize units of Indians for service in Cuba, as did Richard Henry Pratt, the founder of the Carlisle School for Indians. Although Pratt had previously opposed the formation of all-Indian regiments because it flew in the face of his belief that Indians should be fully integrated into American society, he proposed forming a regiment of former Carlisle Indian students. What better way to demonstrate Carlisle's success in preparing Indian youth for their place in American society?

Although none of these proposed units were actually formed, a number of Indians did enlist in Theodore Roosevelt's First Volunteer Regiment, known popularly as the Rough Riders. Indians served in several of the Rough Rider troops, but most were in Troop L, which Roosevelt recruited from the Indian Territory. Although no fan of the red man, Roosevelt nonetheless had high praise for his Indian troopers because they displayed those martial qualities he admired. "We have a number of Indians," he wrote to Henry Cabot Lodge in May 1898, "who are excellent riders and seem to be pretty good fellows."

One of those "good fellows" was William J. Pollock, a Pawnee. Educated at Haskell Institute in Kansas, Pollock was a self-taught artist whose work was later exhibited at the Smithsonian Institution. According to Roosevelt, who wrote about his Indian troopers in his 1899 book *The Rough Riders*, Pollock was "one of the gamest fighters and best soldiers in the regiment [and] . . . among the men whom I noticed as leading in the charges and always being nearest the enemy." When the regiment disbanded after the war, Roosevelt reportedly told him: "Pollock, you are one of the bravest men in my regiment. I

prompted by an increase in enlistments from the immigrant population after the economic depression of 1893. Although most Indians were not U.S. citizens, as a class they were exempt from the law because the Army was conducting a social experiment, in which one outcome was to teach English to Indian recruits. Ironically, the failure of the experiment with all-Indian units meant that individual Indian soldiers would be integrated into the Army, an equal-rights opportunity that eluded black soldiers until WWII. After the experiment ended, most of the Indian soldiers returned to civilian status, although a few remained on military rolls as scouts.

WARRIORS IN UNIFORM

could not wish for a better soldier. I would have liked some more Pawnees like you."

The proof of the success of Roosevelt's charismatic appeal as a leader was that the cowboys in the Rough Riders, many of them former Indian fighters, coexisted peacefully and cooperated well with their Indian comrades. Undoubtedly, Roosevelt spoke the truth when he later claimed that his Indian troopers "lived on terms of complete equality with the whites." Some of the Indians among his Rough Riders were inclined toward wildness, he admitted, but "their wildness was precisely like that of the cowboys with whom they were associated."

Although Indian soldiers also fought in the Philippines and a few fought in the Boxer Rebellion in China, the real change in attitude toward Indians serving in the U.S. armed forces did not come until the outbreak of the First World War.

Choctaw Bankston Johnson was one of Theodore Roosevelt's First Volunteer Regiment in 1898, popularly known as the Rough Riders.

PLAINS LEDGER ART

To Plains Indian warriors, drawing was as natural as fighting. Before paper became available the warriors expressed their artistic creativity on bone, bark, rock walls, and tanned animal hides; but once introduced to paper in the early 19th century, they eagerly adopted the medium. Since the first paper products usually available to them were the large, lined accounting books kept by traders and military officers, their creations are known as ledger art—even though the warrior artists used any paper products that came their way, including diaries, notebooks, Army rosters, and even business flyers. The ledger drawings, which frequently depicted the artist's war deeds, or "coups," were mostly rendered in ink, pencil, or crayon. Shown are three such drawings from a ledger book at the Milwaukee Public Museum that belonged to Sioux warrior Red Hawk. According to a note inside the ledger, Capt. R. Miller originally "captured" the book from Red Hawk at Wounded Knee Creek, South Dakota, on January 8, 1891, days after the massacre at Wounded Knee. The majority of the 105 drawings in the book show warfare and horse capture, particularly between the Sioux and Crow, traditional enemies. In many, one or more of the protagonists are wearing military uniforms, suggesting that they were serving as Army scouts. Differences in artistic style indicate that several warriors besides Red Hawk used the ledger to record their war deeds. The captions may have been written by Captain Miller.

CAPTURES TWO PONIES
The finest coup is capturing an enemy horse, and in the drawing above, Shows the Feather sprints away amid a hail of bullets with two ponies in hand.

KILLS A CROW

Here, a Lakota warrior named Mato Huka shows himself on horseback running down a Crow who shot at him and missed.

PUSHES CROW TO ONE SIDE

In this image Shows the Feather, who has dismounted and holds only a bow and arrow, fearlessly challenges his better-armed Crow adversary.

CHIPPEWA (OJIBWE) INDIANS AND
RETURNED SOLDIERS IN WISCONSIN
POSE AT A WORLD WAR I VICTORY
CELEBRATION IN 1919 WITH THEIR
INTERPRETER (FOREGROUND).

Chapter Three

FIGHTING THE METAL HATS: WORLD WAR I

JAMES BLACK HAWK, A
CHEROKEE, SERVED AS A
FIREMAN SECOND CLASS ON
THE U.S.S. *NORTH DAKOTA*
DURING WORLD WAR I.

The Great War proved a watershed for America's Native peoples. They established a remarkable record of patriotism and selflessness during a conflict they had no apparent reason to join or recognize. Still, they contributed to the victory beyond their tribal numbers and resources.

Several tribes made it "their" war. Most notable was the Onondaga Nation of the once-feared Iroquois Confederacy. It unilaterally declared war on Germany, citing ill-treatment of tribal members performing with a Wild West show and stranded in Berlin when the hostilities began.

A RUSH TO SERVE

Although most Indians in 1917 were not subject to the draft because they were not U.S. citizens, they enlisted in astonishing numbers. Even before the draft registration began, some 2,000 had volunteered, many of them eager to gain "war honors." All told, 17,213 Indians registered for the draft: Of these, 6,509, or 37.6 percent, were inducted, most of them as volunteers. The Passamaquoddy of Maine, one of the numerically smaller tribes in the U.S., fielded 500 volunteers, including their chief, Peter Neptune.

Perhaps more telling, only 228 of the 17,213 Indians who registered for the draft received an exemption—most because of their age. The Bureau of Indian Affairs later declared that of the 10,000 Native Americans who actually served in the Army and the 2,000 who served in the Navy, fully three out of four were volunteers.

These totals do not count Indians like George White Fox, a Crow who changed his name so he could enlist as a citizen. He served as George White on board the U.S.S. *Wyoming* in the North Atlantic during World War I, but when he returned to southern Montana the government refused to recognize his service. When White Fox died, there was no veteran's burial and no flag presented to his widow. His descendants continue to fight for his recognition.

The Indians volunteered and they fought, accumulating casualties and decorations that belied their small numbers. An estimated 5 percent of the Indian doughboys were killed or injured in the Great War compared with a 1 percent casualty rate for the entire American Expeditionary Force, which suffered a total of 50,280 killed and 95,786 wounded. Some tribal groups suffered even higher rates. An estimated 14 percent of the Pawnee soldiers in the AEF became casualties; the various Sioux groups suffered an average casualty rate of 10 percent.

In truth, Army officers motivated by romantic notions of Native Americans' fighting abilities often gave their Indian soldiers the most dangerous assignments. Some Indians, in turn, accepted those assignments to prove their worth as soldiers and to live up to the unrealistic and stereotypical images of their warrior heritage. Nonetheless, some of the Indian soldiers did welcome dangerous duties as opportunities to fulfill their warrior aspirations.

RESISTING CONFINEMENT

Whatever their motivation, Indian doughboys did nothing to tarnish their warrior reputations. According to Maj. Tom Reilly, who commanded the Third Battalion, 165th Infantry Division, "Indians were always at the front. If a battle was on, and you wanted to find the Indians, you would always find them at the front." During the Meuse-Argonne offensive, the first major test for American forces in the war, Major Reilly lost 476 of the 876 men in his battalion. "The Indians in the front ranks were thoroughly swept away," he noted in his report. "When an Indian went down, another Indian immediately stepped to the front."

Historian Brian Dippie estimates that 150 Native Americans earned medals for valor in battle, while ten received the Croix de Guerre, France's highest military award. One decorated war hero was Chauncey Eagle Horn of South Dakota, who was killed in France. His father had fought Custer at the Battle of the Little Bighorn. Joe Young Hawk, the son of one of Custer's Arikara scouts at that battle, was wounded and taken prisoner by the Germans but later escaped after killing three guards and capturing two. Despite gunshot wounds to both legs, Young Hawk marched his prisoners back to American lines.

Perhaps the most brilliant record of the Indian warriors who fought in World War I

Karl May's novels featured Apache warrior Winnetou and his German blood brother.

belongs to Pvt. Joseph Oklahombi, a Choctaw in the 141st Infantry. His exploits rivaled those of the more famous Sgt. Alvin York. Oklahombi received the Croix de Guerre for scrambling across 200 yards of barbed-wire entanglements, wrenching a machine gun from its crew, and then using it to capture 171 German soldiers. He held the position for four days while withstanding a constant artillery barrage, including gas shells.

Some 600 Oklahoma Indians, mostly Choctaw and Cherokee, were assigned to the 142nd Infantry of the 36th Texas-Oklahoma National Guard Division and saw action in France. The soldiers were widely recognized for their contributions in battle, and four received the Croix de Guerre.

Indian soldiers excelled as messengers and scouts. One reason for their success in this regard, it was believed, was an inherent sense of direction. White officers claimed that non-Indian scouts frequently had to consult their compasses when operating at night or in dense forests, exposing themselves to German snipers. Officers of the 142nd Regiment tested this theory by sending five Indians and five non-Indians on a reconnoitering exercise. All the soldiers wore blindfolds. The officers reported

Choctaw soldiers in training to send coded radio and telephone transmissions during World War I were forerunners of the famed code talkers of World War II.

that each of the Indians crawled to his objective, whereas the non-Indians crawled in every direction but the right one.

Because of the Germans' ability to intercept telephone communications, the Allies made frequent use of runners to convey messages. Invariably Indians were chosen for this dangerous duty because of their reputed courage and acclaimed scouting skills. One such messenger was Chester Armstrong Four Bears, a Cheyenne River Sioux, who reached regimental headquarters with his message despite heavy machine gun fire and a poison gas barrage that forced him to crawl most of the way from his front-line trench. Then, ignoring orders to report to

the hospital for examination, he crept back to his unit. Along the way he encountered an injured French messenger who was so grateful to his rescuer that he gave Four Bears the Croix de Guerre pinned to his tunic.

Some of the success of the Indian soldiers can be credited to Germans' fear of "American savages." This fear was instilled by the Wild West shows that had been popular in Europe in the decades immediately preceding the outbreak of the Great War and by the fanciful novels of Karl May, the Zane Grey of Germany. The late 19th-century author wrote a series of novels about the American West that established a deeply romantic and emotional tie to Indians that Germans

WARRIORS IN UNIFORM

MEMBERS OF A CHOCTAW TELEPHONE SQUAD WERE ABLE TO TRANSMIT MESSAGES IN THEIR NATIVE TOUNGE, WHICH WAS AN UNEXPECTED BENEFIT TO THE U.S. ARMY.

Joseph Oklahombi, a Choctaw, was awarded the Croix de Guerre after capturing 171 German soldiers.

Chief Plenty Coups, who had who led the Crow forces at the Battle of the Rosebud in 1876, participates in the dedication ceremonies at the Tomb of the Unknown Soldier 45 years later.

cherish to this day. Adolf Hitler, a Karl May fan, regarded Indians as "red Aryans."

One of May's Indian heroes was an Apache chief named Winnetou. Although May described the Apache as honorable and noble, he also described at length the cruelty they inflicted on their enemies, acts that included torture and scalping. May also extolled the fighting skills of Native Americans, claiming that a warrior could throw a tomahawk with such accuracy that he could cut off the tip of an adversary's finger at a hundred paces. Concern about facing American Indians in combat was so pervasive that the German press denied any were on the western front, while some American officials, hoping to further demoralize the enemy, suggested sending soldiers dressed as Indians on night patrols.

CODE TALKERS OF WWI

An unexpected benefit of the service of uniformed warriors was their role as messengers and telephone operators, because the Germans were unable to understand their languages. In the 142nd Regiment alone were Indians speaking 26 different languages or dialects. The idea originated with officers in that regiment who asked two Choctaw soldiers to transmit messages in their native tongue. Although the use of Native telephone operators was not widespread during World War I, Comanche, Cheyenne, Osage, and Lakota speakers are known to have transmitted messages on the battlefield. One difficulty with the novel arrangement, a precursor of the more organized and well-known Navajo code talking system of World War II, was the

DOUGHBOYS AND PROUD OF IT

The natural world is sacred in traditional Native American culture, and rock formations are considered to be especially powerful. Rock art—pictographs, which are painted on stone, and petroglyphs, which are incised or chipped—can be found throughout the West. South-central Montana boasts one of the largest concentrations of rock art in the United States.

Two warriors from the Crow Nation, James Cooper and Clarence L. Stevens, were working on the Spear-O Ranch near Lodge Grass, Montana, on the Crow Indian Reservation when World War I erupted. The two Native cowboys enlisted together and served in the same unit in France, the Fourth Infantry Division. It was nicknamed the Ivy division for its insignia of four ivy leaves on a diamond field symbolizing the Roman numeral IV.

Cooper was probably the artist for the panel below—the most recent of many Crow warrior biographic pieces at the Joliet archaeological site, in south-central Montana. Both Cooper and Stevens returned to the cowboy life after the Great War. Their descendants are successful ranchers and cowhands. This photograph was taken by Timothy P. McCleary, a professor of history at the Little Bighorn Tribal College on the Crow Reservation.

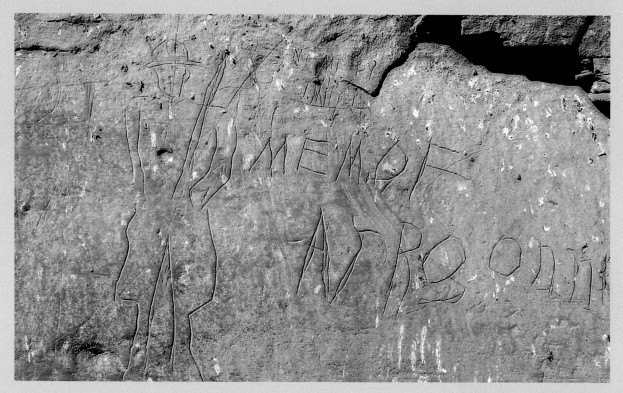

In this rock panel at Joliet archaeological site in south-central Montana, WWI Crow warrior James Cooper chipped a petroglyph commemorating his service.

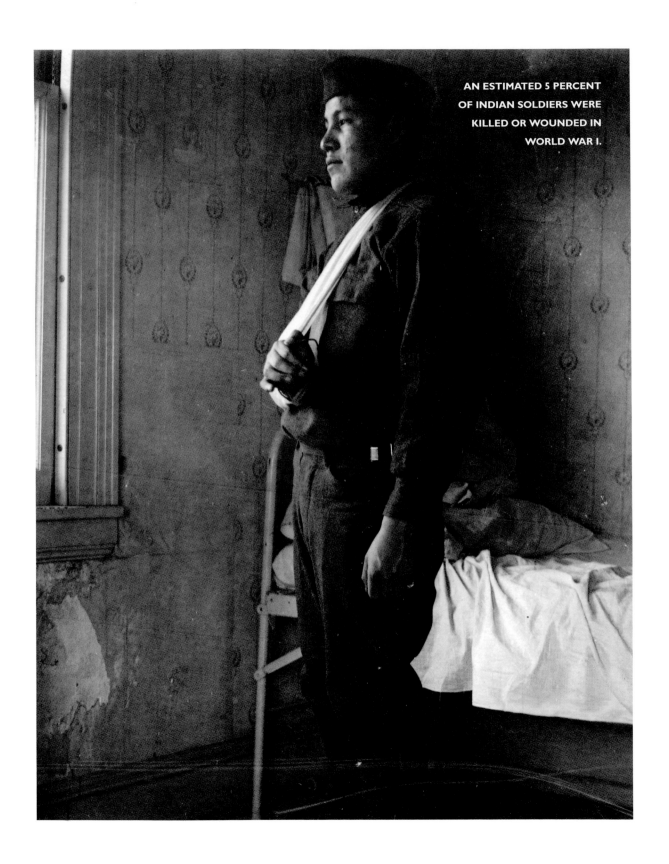

AN ESTIMATED 5 PERCENT
OF INDIAN SOLDIERS WERE
KILLED OR WOUNDED IN
WORLD WAR I.

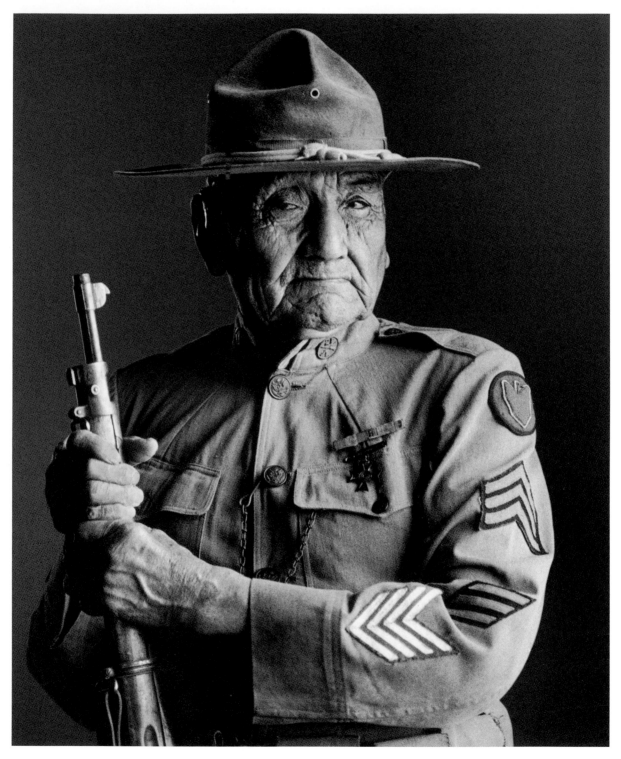

Harvier Adams, a Pima, relives a proud moment as a member of the 158th Infantry, 40th Division—the only all-volunteer Indian unit in World War I.

lack of military words in the Indian vocabulary. The Choctaws devised a workable code: A "big gun" meant artillery, a "tribe" was a regiment, a "grain of corn" was a battalion, a "stone" was a hand grenade, poison gas was "bad air," casualties were "scalps," and a patrol "many scouts."

HOME FRONT SUPPORT

Indians also contributed to home front activities during the war. More than 10,000 joined the Red Cross, and they purchased more than $25 million in Liberty Bonds.

Typical of Indian support at home is the story told of a 75-year-old Ute woman who attended a Red Cross meeting on her reservation. Each finger a person held up meant a $10 donation to the Red Cross. The old woman held up five fingers, which was recorded as a gift of $50. A few days later when she limped to the agency headquarters to sign her contribution form, she became indignant when the interpreter explained she had donated $50. "I want to give $500," she declared. When the reservation superintendent told her she had only $513 to her credit on the agency account books, she smiled: "Thirteen dollars left? That's enough for me."

Perhaps it was recognition by a guilt-ridden country that thousands of noncitizen Indians had fought for the United States during World War I that accounted for the invitation to Chief Plenty Coups, who led the Crow forces at the Battle of the Rosebud, to participate in the dedication ceremonies at the Tomb of the Unknown Soldier on November 11, 1921. Whatever the reason, the choice was a good one. Plenty Coups, acclaimed as the "Chief of all Chiefs," was 70 at the outbreak of the war and too old to enlist, but he not only encouraged his young men to volunteer—some 30 did—but he also kept a large map of France on the wall of his house so he could follow the news of the conflict. "My heart sings with pride when I think of the fighting my people, the red men of all tribes, did in this last great war," Plenty Coups told his biographer, "and if ever the hands of my own people hold the rope that keeps this country's flag high in the air, it will never come down while an Absarokee [Crow] warrior lives."

Plenty Coups was not the only Indian to participate in the formal ceremonies at Arlington Cemetery that blustery November day. One of the pallbearers was Thomas D. Saunders, a Cheyenne from Oklahoma who had received the Croix de Guerre for his exploits during the Great War. But it was Plenty Coups, dressed in full tribal regalia, who captured the attention of the 100,000 spectators. Although he was not scheduled to speak—that honor had been reserved for President Warren G. Harding—the old warrior could not resist making a few remarks as he laid a magnificent Crow war bonnet and coup stick on the casket. Lifting his arms to the heavens and speaking the Crow tongue in a voice filled with emotion, he said:

I feel it an honor to the red man that he takes part in this great event, because it shows that the thousands of Indians who fought in the great war are appreciated by the white man. I am glad to represent all the Indians of the United States in placing on the grave of this noble warrior this coup stick and war bonnet, every eagle feather of which represents a deed of valor by my race. I hope that the Great Spirit will grant that these noble warriors have not given up their lives in vain and that there will be peace to all men hereafter. This is the Indian's hope and prayer.

WARRIORS IN UNIFORM

CHIEF PLENTY COUPS, STANDING WITH THE GROUP AT LEFT, PLACED A WREATH, HIS WAR BONNET, AND HIS COUP STICK AT THE TOMB OF THE UNKNOWN SOLDIER.

NATIVE WOMEN IN THE MILITARY

Pvt. Lori Piestewa (see page 163) may well be the first female American Indian soldier ever to die in battle, although no one knows for sure. According to *Indian Country Today,* the first active-duty Indian women were four Sioux nuns from South Dakota who served as nurses during the Spanish-American War. Originally assigned to the military hospital at Jacksonville, Florida, they were transferred to Savannah, Georgia; then they sailed to Havana, Cuba, where one of them—

Cadet Micah Rae Highwalking, West Point Class of 2010, at the grave of George Armstrong Custer, Class of 1861.

Sister Anthony—died of pneumonia. Although given a military funeral, Sister Anthony was denied burial in Arlington National Cemetery.

During World War I, 14 American Indian women joined the Army Nurse Corps. World War II saw a dramatic increase, with nearly 800 Native American women serving in a variety of capacities, primarily as nurses. American Indian women nurses then served in mobile Army hospitals in both the Korean and Vietnam Wars. That number has swelled dramatically since Vietnam, and American Indian women are now well represented in all of the branches of the armed forces as well as the four service academies. One of those women is Micah Rae Highwalking, a member of the Northern Cheyenne tribe, who entered West Point in 2006.

Says Highwalking, "It is a great honor for me to be representing the Northern Cheyenne people because they are marked with such respect in Indian country for their role in the Battle of Little Bighorn and the Fort Robinson Outbreak. I take great pride in going to school here even though it is sometimes awkward knowing that Custer studied in the same buildings I study in, slept in the same barracks I sleep in, and ate in the same mess hall I eat in every day. But in the end I am comforted because I know that I am now in a position that I can help my people. As the first Northern Cheyenne to be at West Point, I'm now fighting a different war, a war that is taking my people—and all Native Americans—where they have never been.

"My goal is to pave the way for other Northern Cheyenne and Native American students to study at great colleges and academies. In that regard, if someone asks me if I am a warrior in uniform I say, 'Yes, I am.'"

Four Native American members of the Women's Army Auxiliary Corps stand at attention. Several hundred Indian women served in the WACs, WAVEs, and Army Nurse Corps during World War II.

The Women's Memorial at Arlington Cemetery is collecting the oral histories of Native women in the armed forces. Melinda Cain, a Pueblo-Jicarilla Apache, served as an Army specialist from 1987 to 1990. Although celebrated as a member of the military by her male Apache kinfolk, she says her male Pueblo relatives saw the military as strictly a man's world. Cain says that she drew on her Native traditions, such as dance, during boot camp. "The drumbeat of those songs was what I would always hear in my mind as I ran. The drumbeat kept my step in unison with everyone else and gave me strength to keep on," she told an interviewer at the opening of an exhibit associated with the Women's Memorial. Another participant is Iva Good Voice Flute, an Oglala Sioux, who served in the Air Force from 1991 to 1995. She says that although the Air Force treated her as an equal, male veterans on the Pine Ridge Reservation did not. She recalled that while attending a powwow she was not allowed to fold the flag at evening retreat because, although a veteran, she was a woman. "I cannot forget the sting of those words," she said. "The incident changed me." Because of her efforts to change attitudes, though, the tribe has created a drum song specifically for female veterans.

FRIENDSHIP GIFTS

American Indian leaders received a variety of diplomatic gifts intended to earn their friendship and support in the early years of the Republic. These included gorgets, breastplates, silver pipes, and even silver-headed canes that Abraham Lincoln presented to pueblo leaders because canes had been used as symbols of authority by the Spanish when dealing with the Indians of the American Southwest. But the gifts that Indian leaders most prized were weapons like swords, pipe tomahawks, rifles, and pistols. Made specifically for presentation to tribal leaders, even the weapons were engraved with the U.S. eagle and bore phrases and symbols denoting peace and friendship like the two hands clasped in a handshake on the presidential medals. Whether medals, gorgets, tomahawks, or guns, however, these state gifts had one purpose—to attach the tribal leaders to the United States. A Henry repeating rifle that President U.S. Grant gave to a Lakota chief in 1872, now in the National Museum of the American Indian, bears this inscription: "From the President for Bravery & True Friendship."

GORGET
First worn by knights to protect their throats, silver gorgets such as this, from about 1800, became popular uniform accessories with the European military and were prized by Indian leaders.

VICTORY GIFT
General "Mad Anthony" Wayne presented this richly embossed pipe tomahawk to the Miami chief Little Turtle in 1795, at the signing of the Treaty of Greenville after his victory over the Ohio tribes at the Battle of Fallen Timbers.

IN FRIENDSHIP
This silver-plated tomahawk engraved with the clasped hands of friendship is typical of the gifts goverment officials presented Indian leaders. win their friendship.

PIPE
Also engraved with the clasped hands of friendship, this silver pipe was another kind of offering the government gave to tribes in the spirit of peace.

AMONG THE MARINES RAISING THE
FLAG ON MOUNT SURIBACHI IN 1945
WAS PIMA IRA HAYES.

Chapter Four

FIGHTING THE METAL HATS: WORLD WAR II

MEMBERS OF THE STANDING ROCK SIOUX NATION—BOTH SUN DANCERS AND UNIFORMED MILITARY PERSONNEL—SALUTE THE FLAG AT SUNRISE CEREMONIES IN LITTLE EAGLE, SOUTH DAKOTA, IN 1942.

After the Great War, Indians continued to enlist in the armed forces. At least 4,000 were in uniform in the Army, Navy, Air Force, Coast Guard, and National Guard before Pearl Harbor. Immediately upon the declaration of war, Indians rushed to enlist. Half the eligible males on some reservations volunteered for duty. Several tribes held special war councils to prepare for mobilization. The Navajo Tribal Council, for one, called a special convention in January 1942. With 50,000 tribal members in attendance the council declared its support for the war effort and promised to stand firm with the United States "until this nation shall achieve final, complete, and lasting victory."

A FERVOR TO SERVE

Although as many as 45 percent of Navajo volunteers were rejected because of health and literacy requirements, some 3,600—fully 6 percent of the tribal population—served on active duty. Navajo men were so eager to join the fight, some arrived at registration centers with their rifles and shotguns. At Fort Defiance, volunteers stood in the snow for hours to sign their draft cards. Nearly one-fourth of the 3,600 Ramah Navajo enlisted the day after war was declared.

The same fervor was seen throughout Indian country. One-fourth of the Mescalero Apache enlisted. At the Lac Oreilles Reservation in Wisconsin, 100 Chippewa men enlisted from a population of 1,700, and at Grand Portage nearly all the eligible Chippewa men enlisted. At Fort Peck in Montana 131 Blackfeet volunteered. Even the

Hopi, whose members shared a historical suspicion of the white world, contributed 213 men, or 10 percent of their population of 2,205, to the armed forces.

A common misunderstanding among the Indian volunteers was the expectation that everyone who registered for the draft would be called into service. Many were turned down, though, for age or health reasons.

"I [was] rejected seven times on account of having old," a Pima man complained. "I am only 37 years old." Another Arizona Indian, rejected for being overweight, argued, "Don't want to run. Want to fight." A Chippewa man, rejected because he had no teeth, is said to have snarled, "I don't want to bite 'em. I just want to shoot 'em!" Also ridiculed was the idea of entering a draft lottery. "Since when has it been necessary to draw lots for a fight?" was a frequent joke in Indian country.

By 1942, at least 99 percent of all eligible Indian males had registered for the draft. Had all eligible American males enlisted in the same proportion as tribal people, there would have been no need for the Selective Service System. The Bureau of Indian Affairs later reported that, exclusive of officers, 24,521 reservation Indians saw military service during the war. About 20,000 nonreservation Indians also served. In other words, something like 45,000 Indians, more than 10 percent of the entire estimated population of 350,000 Indians in the United States, saw active duty in the armed forces during World War II. In some tribes, up to 70 percent of the men were in the military. And hundreds of Indian women served, as well, in

About 20 Percent of the Indian Population… Joined the Fight Against Adolf Hitler.

the Women's Army Corps (WACs), the Navy's Women Accepted for Voluntary Emergency Service (WAVES), and the Army Nurse Corps.

All told, counting the Indians who worked in the defense industry as well as those who joined the armed forces, about 20 percent of the Indian population, or 65,000 men and women, joined the fight against Adolf Hitler, a man they called "He Who Smells His Moustache," and Benito Mussolini, whom they dubbed "Gourd Chin." American Indians also invested more than $50 million in war bonds and contributed generously to the Red Cross and to relief societies for the Army and Navy. It was a remarkable show of loyalty on the part of a people who had lost almost all but their pride, dignity, and warrior spirit at the hands of the federal government.

CODE TALKERS OF WWII

The most celebrated of the World War II warriors in uniform were the code talkers, Indians who communicated messages on the battlefield in their tribal languages. Building on the success of the Choctaw message transmitters of World War I, the American military made extensive use of speakers of Native languages in World War II. Although several tribes participated in the program, including Hopi, Comanche, Cherokee, and Chippewa speakers, the most celebrated and publicized were the Navajo code talkers.

John Goodluck, Sr., one of the code talkers, recalled a test conducted on the reservation for Navy officials, who were somewhat skeptical about using Indians to send secret communications. For the test, he said, the military placed

radios 300 to 400 yards apart and sent coded messages using both Navajo code talkers and regular Morse code machines. "The code talkers deciphered the message in under a minute; the machines took an hour," Goodluck laughed.

Code talker messages were strings of seemingly unrelated Navajo words. The code talkers would translate each word into English and then decipher the message by using only the first letter of each English word. For example, several Navajo words could be used to represent the letter *a—wol-la-chee* (ant), *be-la-sana* (apple), and *tse-nill* (ax). Although the Navajo used more than one word to represent letters, about 450 common military terms had no equivalent and so had assigned code words. For example, "division" was *ashih-hi* (salt); "America" was *Ne-he-mah* (Our mother); "fighter plane" was *da-he-tih-hi* (hummingbird); "submarine" became *besh-lo* (iron fish); and "tank destroyer" was *chay-da-gahi-nail-tsaidi* (tortoise killer).

Eventually, 379 Navajo code talkers served in the Pacific theater. "Some say there were 400, but many failed. You had to know both English and Navajo," said Goodluck, who served in the Third Marine Division from March 1943 to December 1945 and participated in the invasions of Guadalcanal and Bougainville in the Solomon Islands; in Guam; and in Iwo Jima, Japan.

Code talkers from other tribes also served in the European theater. Charles Chibitty, the last survivor of the Comanche code talkers, who died in July 2005, said two Comanche were assigned to each of the Fourth Infantry Division's three regiments. They sent coded messages from the front line to division headquarters, where other Comanche decoded them. Chibitty, who joined the Army in January 1941 along with 17 other Comanches, said they compiled a 100-word vocabulary of military terms during basic training at Fort Benning, Georgia. "Machine gun" became "sewing machine," Chibitty recalled, "because of the noise the sewing machine made when my mother was sewing." Since there was no Comanche word for "tank," the code talkers used their word for "turtle." "Bomber" became "pregnant airplane." "Hitler" was *posah-tai-vo,* or "crazy white man." Chibitty recalled that the first message he sent on D-Day, using the code the Comanche had created was, after translation into English, "Five miles to the right of the designated area and five miles inland the fighting is fierce and we need help."

Fortunately, the Bureau of Indian Affairs had not yet succeeded in eradicating Indian languages, a fact not lost on Kevin Gover, Assistant Secretary of the Interior for Indian Affairs, who spoke at a ceremony honoring the code talkers in 1999. "It's a great irony," he said, "that in just two or three generations of being in conflict with the United States, our warriors would go forward and play such a crucial role in the victory over this country's enemies."

AN HONORABLE WARRIOR

If the code talkers as a group were the most celebrated warriors in uniform in World War II, the best known individual was Pima Ira Hamilton

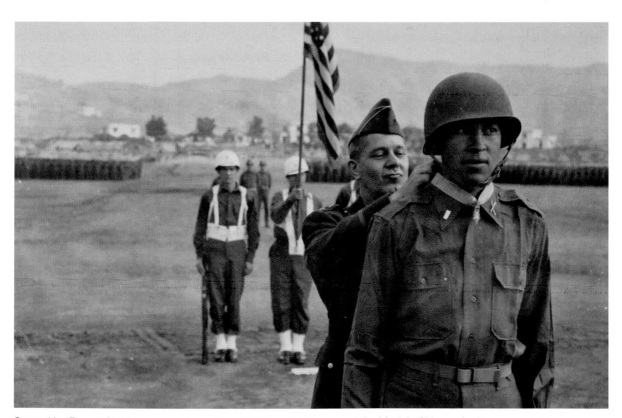

Second Lt. Ernest Childers, a member of the "Fighting 45th," received the Medal of Honor for his service in Italy.

A MUSCOGEE THUNDERBIRD
IN WORLD WAR II

The Germans had been told that the Forty-fifth Infantry was a National Guard outfit manned largely by Red Indians, racially inferior people who had no love of the white man and probably wouldn't fight. How wrong they were.

—Eric Morris, *Circles of Hell: The War in Italy, 1943-1945*

My father, Freeland E. Douglas (Hodulgee Muscogee), was one of those 45th Infantry Division "Red Indians" whose warrior skills were underestimated by the Germans. He and all the original soldiers of Company C, 180th Regiment, were tribal citizens and students of Chilocco Indian School in Oklahoma. All were highly decorated and one Muscogee (Creek) Chiloccoan, Ernest Childers, was the first American Indian to win the Medal of Honor. The 45th was one of four National Guards activated in 1940 by President Franklin D. Roosevelt in anticipation of American entry into the war in Europe.

Dad entered the 45th Division's Oklahoma National Guard in September 1940 and fought in North Africa, Sicily, and southern Italy. He served his unit until he was wounded in combat near Monte Cassino in January 1944. He was air vacced to a hospital in Libya, where his legs were saved, and sailed home on the hospital ship, the *Seminole*. After numerous operations, he returned to Chilocco for his senior year. In graduation remarks, Chilocco Superintendent L. E. Correll told the Chilocco Class of '46, "You have lost fully one third of your original class who should be graduating with you this spring." The toll on the Classes of '39 to '45 was even greater. After school in 1947, Dad became the first person in Oklahoma to reenlist in the U.S. Army under a new law for disabled veterans.

In 1956, Dad took our family to Monte Cassino and Nettuno, Italy, to pay tribute to all those who did not survive World War II. He was stationed with Allied Forces Southern Italy, NATO, and we lived in Naples. Europe was still recovering from the war at that time and there were many families living in caves in the Neapolitan hills. We drove the 50 miles north of Naples to Monte Cassino on the same road Dad had inched along in the 1940s. He marveled at how fast we had made the trip and at the serenity of the sloping green hillsides and the gleaming monastery on high that the Germans held to stop the Allied Forces from marching to Rome.

It is estimated that over 350,000 people died between January and May 1944 in the four battles for Monte Cassino. The Allies were from America, Britain, Canada, France, India, Poland, and South Africa; they were Gurkhas of Nepal, Goumiers of Morocco, Maoris of New Zealand, Aboriginals of Australia, and Sikhs of the Punjab; they were American Negroes who couldn't vote at home, and Japanese Americans whose relatives were in internment camps, some of them on Indian reservations. Like Dad, many of the 45th American Indians from Arizona, Colorado, New Mexico, and Oklahoma were fresh from the brutal "civilizing" programs of federal Indian boarding schools. Unlike the German intelligence suggested, however, they fought until they gained ground or had nothing else to give.

We followed Dad through the memorials, monuments, and immaculate British and Polish cemeteries, calling the names of Dad's relatives and friends who died there but were buried somewhere else and nowhere. We sat by the clear Rapido River, which he said ran red with blood in 1944. We listened to his remembrances of the bravery and good humor of boys he'd known since childhood and those he met on troop ships crossing the Atlantic and Mediterranean, in the sands of North Africa; and in the mud and foxholes of Italy. We left our offerings of tobacco, cedar, and sage, saving certain medicines for Dad's fellow Creeks and his and Mom's Chilocco

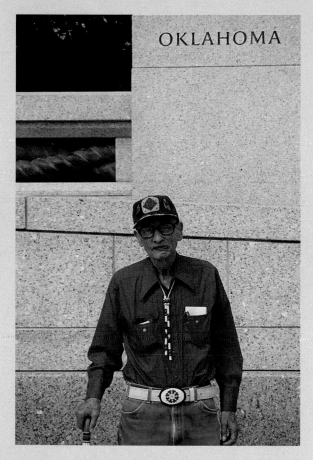

Freeland E. Douglas served in the 45th Infantry Division.

classmates. We stayed in the town of Cassino that night. I was 11 and my twin brothers were 6. We played with kids our age while our parents visited with townspeople about the war. Every so often, the grown-ups had tears in their eyes.

The next day, we drove 50 miles west to visit the Sicily-Rome American Cemetery and Memorial, which had opened in Nettuno, near Anzio and 40 miles south of Rome. We got there before dawn so we could start the day with the proper prayers for all those who died in the bloody battles. We walked through the gleaming white grave markers of carved marble crosses and Stars of David, stopping for Dad to say something about people and places. We sang two warrior songs and a song for the beauty of Mother Earth growing from her children.

We left medicine for everyone in Dad's unit and other heroes he knew. We searched for names on the walls honoring more than 3,000 Americans who died in combat but have no graves. Some names we never found anywhere. Those names of the missing are etched in the walls of white marble from Carrara, the same glistening marble Michelangelo famously used for his commemorative sculptures. I remember some of those names to this day.

Dad had nightmares about events and sights and smells of war, but he always took pride in having been a warrior. The 45th insignia is the Thunderbird, a great sky spirit. Its design was adapted from its first emblem, one used for millennia as a tribal symbol for peace until it was co-opted by the Nazis as their symbol of hate. Dad beaded the Thunderbird on a baseball cap and wore it with pride until his passing in April 2007 at age 85.

—*Suzan Shown Harjo*

Hayes, one of the Marines who helped raise the American flag on Iwo Jima. At the age of 19, he left school to enlist in the Marine Corps. His tribal chairman told him to be an "Honorable Warrior" and bring honor upon his family. Dubbed Chief Falling Cloud at the U.S. Marine Corps parachutist school at San Diego, California, Hayes was assigned to a parachute battalion of the Fleet Marine Force upon graduation. As luck would have it, he found himself part of the American invasion force that attacked the Japanese stronghold of Iwo Jima. There, on February 23, 1945, he and five others—four Marines and a Navy corpsman—raised the U.S. flag atop Mount Suribachi in a dramatic moment captured for posterity by combat photographer Joe Rosenthal. Three of the flag raisers died in the continued fighting on the island, and the corpsman was wounded.

Rosenthal's photograph captured the American imagination, and, hoping to capitalize on

PVT. WALLACE GRANT, A PIMA AND COMPETITIVE RUNNER, TRANSPORTS A MESSAGE FROM A SCOUTING PATROL TO THE MAIN LINE OF RESISTANCE IN NEW GUINEA.

the dramatic moment, President Harry S. Truman summoned Hayes back to the United States to aid a war bond drive. Hayes was acclaimed an American hero, but he felt he had done nothing heroic. "How could I feel like a hero," he lamented, "when only five men in my platoon of 45 survived, when only 27 men in my company of 250 managed to escape death or injury?" Instead of being shuttled from city to city for publicity purposes, Hayes simply wanted to return to the war. "Sometimes I wish that guy had never made that picture," he confessed.

After the war, Hayes tried to lead an anonymous life on the reservation, but it was impossible. "I kept getting hundreds of letters," he said. "And people would drive through the reservation, walk up to me and ask, 'Are you the Indian who raised the flag on Iwo Jima?'" Alcohol became his only escape. "I was sick," he explained. "I guess I was about to crack up thinking about all my good buddies. They were better men than me and they're not coming back, much less back to the White House, like me."

Never married, and unable to get his life back in balance, Hayes died of exposure in January 1955 at the age of 32. Sadly, he died just ten weeks after attending the dedication ceremony in Washington, D.C., for the U.S. Marine Corps War Memorial, featuring the cast bronze replica of the photograph that had caused him so much pain and torment. Characterized by his Pima people as "a hero to everyone but himself," Corporal Hayes is buried in Arlington Cemetery, just a short distance away from the Iwo Jima Memorial.

Ira Hayes, like most of his American Indian comrades in arms, earned no medals for his battlefield exploits. In fact, of the 464 Medals of Honor—"for gallantry above and beyond the call of duty"—awarded to soldiers during World War II, only 5 went to Native Americans. Three of those so honored were in the same unit, the Fighting 45th: Lt. Jack Montgomery, a Cherokee; Lt. Ernest Childers, a Creek; and Lt. Van Barfoot, a Choctaw. They fought in Italy, and all three survived the war. The 45th Division was a reserve division from Oklahoma and New Mexico. Native Americans from some 50 different tribes made up the vast majority of its troops. The unit's distinctive patch bore a gold thunderbird on a red background in tribute to its Indian personnel. The other two Indian Medal of Honor recipients were Navy Commander Ernest Evans and Pvt. John Reese, Jr., who fought and died in the Philippines.

WARRIOR ARTIST

One of the lesser-known heroes of the Fighting 45th was Brummett Echohawk, a Pawnee who

An all-Navajo Marine Corps unit poses in Peleliu in 1944. Navajo code talkers served in the Pacific, taking part in every assault by the U.S. Marines from 1942 to 1945.

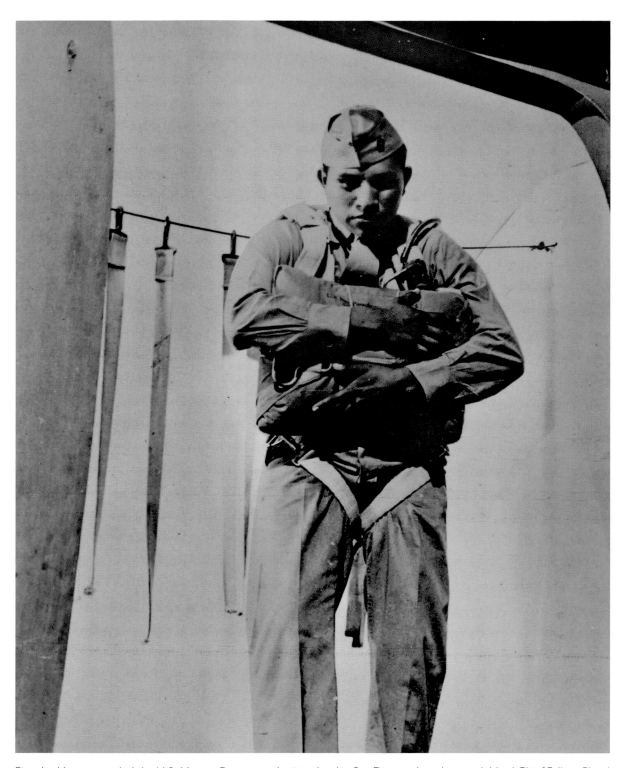

Pima Ira Hayes attended the U.S. Marine Corps parachutist school in San Diego, where he was dubbed Chief Falling Cloud.

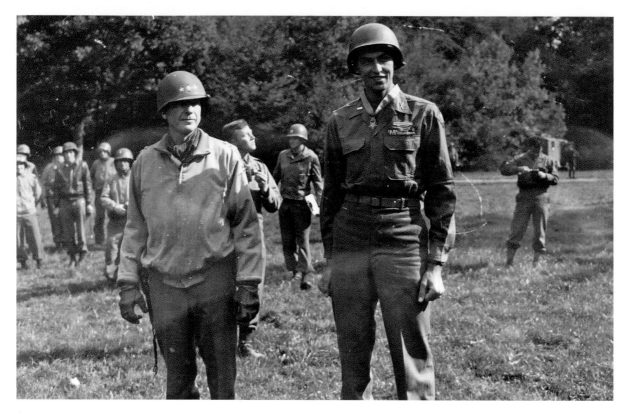

Van Barfoot, a Choctaw who fought with the Fighting 45th, was one of five Native American Medal of Honor recipients in World War II.

earned three Purple Hearts and three Bronze Stars for his exploits in Italy during World War II. After the war he became one of Oklahoma's best known artists, a talent he perfected during lulls on the battlefields of Italy.

Echohawk began sketching the war while in Sicily. "On about the first day," he wrote in his unpublished memoirs, entitled *The Quill of the Thunderbird,* "I found drawing paper and pencils in a battered enemy garrison. From that day forward, I sketched the war. I used the back of a mess kit lid as a drawing board. I did not show off my drawings, for we were all sick of seeing the dead, bloated bodies, in the hot Sicilian sun. Most of the sketching was done during a lull, or when in battalion reserve. I carried my drawing paper in an empty 60-mm waterproof carton.

The small tubular carton fit snugly in my combat pack." When drawing soldiers, he frequently made two sketches, one for his model and one for himself. He even gave copies to German prisoners that he sketched.

Echohawk's drawings became public—and his career as an artist was launched—while he was recuperating from injuries in an Army hospital and a war correspondent discovered them. As a result, the Newspaper Enterprise Association bought several of his drawings and distributed them to its client newspapers in the States. *The Yank,* the official Army newspaper, also published some of his work. Because constant fighting left little time for drawing, he later joked in a 2007 interview with *Tulsa World,* "I became the fastest pen in the West."

But Echohawk first aspired to be a warrior, not an artist, when he dropped out of high school in 1940 at age 17 and joined the National Guard. "When I was young, growing up in Pawnee, Oklahoma," he wrote, "I used to listen to old-time Pawnee Indians tell stories of warriors and battles on the Great Plains. When a warrior distinguished himself in battle, the people gave him a name with great ceremony. The name was one of honor. Songs were composed describing his feats of bravery. Kept as history, the songs were handed down from generation to generation. The warrior was held in honor all his life because he had defended his people and country. My grandfather had been a great warrior. He died when I was two years old; however, I got to see other old Pawnee warriors. In their twilight years, they still carried themselves proud.

Seeing them and respecting them, I wanted very much to be a warrior myself."

As a sergeant in Company B of the 179th Regimental Combat Team, an all-Indian unit from Pawnee, Oklahoma, Echohawk fulfilled his dream. He was part of the American force that landed in Sicily and then stormed ashore at Anzio, considered a turning point in the victory of the Allies in World War II.

"We Indians are in the first wave at Anzio," Echohawk wrote. "I have a sapper team. Our job is to blow beach obstacles and pill boxes. Our barge carries thirty-six men and a Medic. He is a full blood Choctaw Indian. We call him 'Medicine Man.' In the first three days of fighting, I fire 195 rounds of ammo and throw eleven hand grenades. We make bayonet charges with the wild assortment of war cries. I shall

Indian soldiers are (left to right): Robert Dray, a Creek, Lloyd Yellowhorse, a Pawnee, and Olson Damon, a Navajo.

NAVAJO MEMBERS OF THE
158TH U.S. INFANTRY STATIONED ON
THE SOLOMON ISLANDS TAKE PART IN
A TRADITIONAL CEREMONY.

always remember the fear-struck faces of the enemy when closing on them. While attacking an enemy strong point, in one fight, one of my men had the calf of his leg shredded by a 'potato masher' hand grenade. Another took a bad concussion hit. I had my shirt pocket shot off. I crawled through cactus to get behind the enemy. They didn't think a man could crawl through cactus, but they didn't know Indians. I was bloody and cut when I got there, but I destroyed the enemy gun emplacement with a grenade and my bayonet and I counted coup, like a Pawnee warrior."

His memoirs are filled with exploits that sparkle with Indian humor, bravado, and audacity. "On one night patrol we covered 16 miles, running. We guided on the North Star and the mountain winds. An Apache can run fifty miles. A Pawnee can run a hundred. And a Comanche can run down a horse. That night we got behind German armor. We even walked among them in the dark. We got the information we needed. We also took a few bottles of their strong drink and a loaf of their 'saw dus' bread."

Echohawk also told of the fear that the Germans had of American Indians, perhaps a lingering legacy of the Karl May novels. "The 179th RCT takes a fanatical German counterattack. We are shoved back but stop them at the Sele River. We capture prisoners. These troops are fresh. Cocky and arrogant, they sit behind us with hands on their heads singing. Things look dark. In between spirited songs, the prisoners snicker, confident that we will be overrun. Two Indian Military Policemen come to collect prisoners. One is a Pawnee. The other is a Sioux. Both stand at six foot six. They lumber toward the singing German soldiers. Both draw their bayonets. The Sioux growls: 'We American Indians . . . you understand? *Vrstehen?*' They not only understand, they almost have heart failure. One cries hysterically, 'Geneva Convention! Geneva Convention!'"

But the lighthearted moments were few and far between. "Anzio was a nightmare—a complete nightmare," he wrote. It also ended his military career. "With leg and foot wounds, and having taken concussion hits that left me with internal injuries and a partial loss of hearing, I was furloughed home to Pawnee, Oklahoma. There I met Phillip Shield Chief, our platoon sergeant. He had lost an arm. Also there was Sergeant Good Buffalo from our platoon. He had suffered a wound in the temple and ear. While we were home together, the Pawnee tribe honored us as true warriors. A song was composed in our honor. And we were accorded another honor—awarding each of us with a warrior's name."

Ernest Childers, Phillip Gover, Grant Gover, and Brummett Echohawk go through training before the 45th shipped out.

The ceremony for these three Pawnee "Thunderbirds" was held on the Oklahoma prairie under brush arbors on a warm summer day. Several Indian ponies grazed in the distance. When the old chiefs and the other members of the Ahrooks-pakoo-tah, the Warriors Society, brought the American flag into the circle, the spectators rose for the singing of the Pawnee Flag Song. The old warriors, resplendent in fine beadwork, buckskins, and eagle feathers, stood erect although some were bent with age.

"I swelled with pride," Echohawk recalled the ceremony. "My combat art was being published all over the country. And now my tribe was honoring me as a full-fledged warrior."

But then the mood of the ceremony took on a somber feel. Echohawk remembered how the drumbeat slowed, the singers wailed a somber war song, and the elderly onlookers all bowed their heads. Shield Chief's family and relatives began to cry. He asked Good Buffalo whose war song was being sung and learned it belonged to Grant Shield Chief, who was Phillip's brother and a sergeant in their Third Platoon. Good Buffalo whispered to Echohawk that Grant had been killed in southern France.

"My chin dropped. Tears came. According to Pawnee legend, as the Old Ones always said,

BUT WHICH RACE SHALL I BE CALLED?

Indians in the military in World War I were classified as white, except in the segregated South, where they were classified as "colored." Lt. Col. Mark Smith of the U.S. Military Academy, pictured at a powwow, wrote this poem for "those of mixed blood who are more Native in culture and thought than the race they are frequently called."

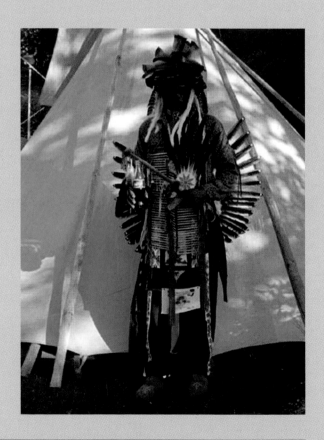

. . . but which race shall I be called?
The recorder says: white, yellow, red, black.
. . . but I have two parents.
The recorder says: white, yellow, red, black
. . . but my parents are from different heritage.
The recorder says: white, yellow, red, black.
. . . but which race shall I be called?
The recorder says: whichever is darker.
. . . that which is darker I am called.

Lt. Col. Mark Smith in ceremonial dress at a powwow.

WARRIORS IN UNIFORM

in every major battle one of us would go. This is not something bad. It is nature's way. All life starts again. So the Old Ones told us before we went overseas. In the creator's plan no life is ever wasted. We accept this. And our fathers and grandfathers of the Warrior Society drilled into us that we are Pawnees: Chaticks—Si-Chaticks, Men of Men. When a warrior falls all birds and animals mourn. This time it was Grant. And I had done a sketch of him. Sniffing, I stood erect and gazed at the American flag snapping in the summer breeze. The low singing continued. From the distant hillside came the whinny of a stud horse. My thoughts went back to Sicily and Italy and our bayonet charges. Then from the peaceful fields of the Pawnee Nation came the sweet call of a bobwhite."

The actual number of Indians who served during World War II is impossible to determine because they were classified as "white" inductees and because many kept their ethnicity to themselves. In the segregated South, though, some Indians were classified as "colored" and assigned to all-black units. In fact, three members of the Rappahannock tribe of Virginia were sentenced to six months in prison for refusing to report to a black induction station at Fort Meade, Maryland. Although they had registered for the draft as Indians, the state cited a study that concluded, "There is not a native-born Virginian claiming to be an Indian who is not mixed with Negro blood and who is not classified as Negro under the laws of this state."

Of the known Indians in the various branches of the armed forces during World War II, 550 were killed—the first one died at Pearl Harbor—and more than 700 were wounded. To those warriors in uniform, the United States awarded 71 Air Medals, 34 Distinguished Flying Crosses, 51 Silver Stars, 47 Bronze Stars, and 5 Medals of Honor.

THE WARRIOR SPIRIT

Most of the Indians who fought and were wounded or who died on the far-flung battlefields of World War II were nameless and forgotten to the vast majority of Americans, but not to their fellow tribesmen, who honored them for their military service and often revered them afterward. This was especially true with tribes in which the warrior spirit has been predominant, such as the Crow Nation of Montana.

Andrew Bird-in-Ground was one of these unsung warrior heroes. During the Allied landing in Normandy, he earned the Bronze Star with three clusters. His Crow people felt he would have received the Medal of Honor but for the fact that he was an Indian. When Bird-in-Ground returned from the war he was given a new name, Kills Many Germans, in recognition of his battlefield bravery. Bird-in-Ground himself was very modest about his exploits. He explained that he fought so hard "because my address at the time I enlisted was in Oregon. I was afraid if I were killed in combat, they would not bury me on the Crow Reservation in Montana. I was not trying to be a hero."

He was a hero to his people, nonetheless. Shortly after returning from the war, Bird-in-Ground was visited by the worried parents of a newborn son, Kenneth Old Coyote. Old Coyote, they said, was critically ill and was not expected to live. They appealed to Bird-in-Ground to visit their son in the Billings hospital and pray for him. His having survived such a terrible battle, they said, made it obvious that God had blessed him, perhaps had given him special powers. Would he try to help their son? Bird-in-Ground visited and prayed over Old Coyote; he also gave him his new name, Kills Many Germans. Twenty years later, during the Vietnam War, Kills Many Germans earned the

"We Were Raised to Be Warriors but...Expected to Succeed in the White Man's World."

Bronze Star himself for saving two wounded comrades while under fire.

Like the Indian doughboys of the Great War, the Native Americans who fought in the Second World War had to cope with a great deal of stereotypical attitudes and language, because most of the non-Natives they encountered had never even met an Indian before. Everything about them aroused curiosity, comment, and confusion, even their names. When Charles Kills the Enemy reported to his induction center and gave his name, he was told to get serious and give his real name. "But Kills the Enemy is my name," he tried to explain. Then there was the hospital nurse who, after checking the chart of a wounded soldier, exclaimed, "How on earth did you get shot with two arrows?" The soldier replied, "That's my name, not my injury."

Invariably, Indian soldiers were called Chief or Geronimo by white comrades. The Indians usually took no offense, since they realized the nicknames were intended not as racial insults but as an acknowledgment of their reputed fighting abilities.

But of the many cultural differences between the Native and non-Native soldiers, few seemed more mysterious and impenetrable than the various purification and blessing ceremonies that were such an important part of Native life. These ceremonies and the blessed objects the Indian soldiers carried—like feathers, medicine bundles, sweet grass, cedar, and other sacred objects—gave the owners peace of mind as they faced the perils of combat. Then, on returning home, other ceremonies purged the Indian

veterans of the mental demons that often tormented non-Indian veterans. Members of numerous tribes held traditional ceremonies before going into combat. Many of these ceremonies were dances intended to weaken the enemy, such as ceremonies held on Pavavu Island after its capture from the Japanese. In one such ceremony, two Oklahoma Indians slashed pictures of Hitler and Japanese Prime Minister Hideki Tojo with their knives at the end of the dance. Six Navajo code talkers also conducted a private ceremony intended to restore harmony.

Before the invasion of Okinawa, war correspondent Ernie Pyle, with the Marine Corps' First Division, filed a story about the unit's eight Navajo code talkers. "The Indian boys knew before we got to Okinawa that the invasion landing wasn't going to be very tough," Pyle wrote. "They were the only ones in the convoy who did know it. For one thing they saw signs and for another they used their own influence."

The "influence" was a ceremony witnessed by a "grave audience" of several thousand Marines. The face-painted Navajo Marines wore outfits fashioned from colored cloth contributed by the Red Cross and adorned with chicken feathers, sea shells, coconuts, and empty cartridge cases that jingled like bells as they danced and sang. Empty ration cans served as drums. The dancers told Pyle that they had asked "the great gods in the sky to sap the Japanese of their strength for this blitz. They put the finger of weakness on them."

The Marines did, in fact, have an easy landing on Okinawa, but things quickly got rough. "What about your little ceremony? What do you call this?" a Marine asked one of the code talkers as they hunkered down in a foxhole. "This is different," the Navajo answered with a smile. "We only prayed for an easy landing."

This was not the only ceremony performed by Native American Marines before and after the conquest of Okinawa. In a special edition of the magazine *Indians at Work* entitled *Indians at War,* mention is made of Apache, Comanche, Crow, Kiowa, Navajo, Pima, and Pueblo tribal members performing the Devil Dance, the Eagle Dance, the Hoop Dance, the War Dance, and the Mountain Chant.

In addition to conducting public ceremonies, many Indian soldiers also carried some type of personal "medicine" and credited these sacred objects with keeping them safe during the war. For instance, when Germans captured Frankie Redbone, a Kiowa, in 1944, his captors told him to put all his belongings on a table. Upon noticing a small pouch in the pile, a German guard asked what it contained. "Indian medicine," Redbone said. The guard, who probably had enjoyed Karl May's Indian novels, took everything but the pouch, and Redbone credited his medicine bundle for enabling him to survive his eight months as a prisoner of war.

MODERN-DAY CROW WARRIOR

The experiences of Joseph Medicine Crow can be seen as typical of Indian soldiers in the World War II era. Born on the Crow Reservation in Montana in 1913, Medicine Crow had been raised by pre-reservation-era grandparents to be tough and strong like traditional Plains Indian warriors. "All the boys my age on the reservation were brought up in two ways at the same time," he said. "We were raised to be warriors but we were also expected to succeed in the white man's world."

The first male Crow to graduate from college—Bacone College in Oklahoma, a four-year

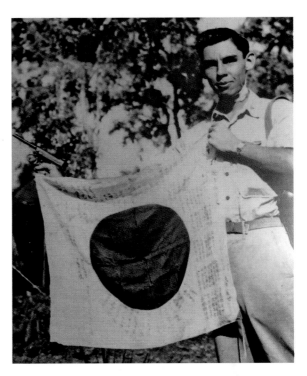

Lt. Woody J. Cochran, a Cherokee and a much-decorated bomber pilot, holds a Japanese flag while serving in New Guinea.

liberal arts college with historic ties to the Native American community—and the first to obtain a master's degree, he was working on his doctorate when World War II interrupted his studies. Although offered a commission in the Army because of his academic background, Medicine Crow turned it down on the grounds that a warrior must first prove himself on the battlefield before leading others into battle. "It was the worst mistake I ever made," he laughed, "because the U.S. Army didn't work on the principles of the Crow tribe and I never got another chance at a commission. I went into the Army a private and came out a private."

Now 94, he lives with his wife Gloria in the town of Lodge Grass, Montana, on the Crow Reservation. The official historian of the Crow tribe, he is the author of several books, which include *Counting Coup,* in which he describes his upbringing as a traditional warrior.

Descended from a long line of famous Crow war chiefs including White Man Runs Him and Medicine Crow, Private Medicine Crow distinguished himself on the battlefields of Germany, where he counted coup on a German soldier and even captured a herd of horses from the Waffen SS. "While serving as an infantryman in Germany," he said, "I was able to perform the four types of war deeds, or 'coups,' a warrior needed to earn in order to become a chief." The most significant of these, he says, was to "sneak into an enemy camp at night, capture a prized horse, and then bring it back home."

The other coups, Medicine Crow explained, were "to touch a fallen enemy, to capture a weapon from an enemy, and to lead a successful war party . . . one in which the goals had been achieved and all the members returned safely. To become a Crow chief, a warrior had to perform at least one of each."

When Medicine Crow went to Germany, though, he did not think in terms of counting coup. "I believed those days were gone," he said. "Naturally, however, I thought about the famous Crow warriors of the past, of my grandfather Medicine Crow who was one of the most famous of our war chiefs. I knew I had a legacy to live up to. My goal was to be a good soldier, to perform honorably in combat if the occasion should occur." When he returned from Germany, though, and the elders asked him and the other Crow warriors to tell their war stories, "lo and behold—I had fulfilled the four requirements to be a chief."

Medicine Crow accomplished his first coup in January 1945, when the Allies began their

A two-man team of Navajo code talkers attached to a Marine regiment relays orders over a field radio in the Pacific.

WARRIORS IN UNIFORM

push into Germany from France. "The ground was covered with snow," Medicine Crow said, and "the boundary that separated the two countries at this point was a little creek, about the size of Lodge Grass Creek, running through a canyon." The canyon was deep and had steep walls. "It was not rocky like our canyons in Montana," Medicine Crow said, "but it had real sharp hills. . . . The French Maginot Line, with its big guns, was behind us. On the other side of this creek, facing us, was the German Siegfried line, with its big guns."

By late afternoon, Medicine Crow and his fellow soldiers had gone down the hill on the French side, crossed into Germany, and started toward the Siegfried line. "Before long," he said, "we ran into foxholes just loaded with Germans," and fighting broke out. Although it soon got dark, the Americans pushed forward, with the Germans slowly withdrawing up the side of their hill toward their big guns. "As they retreated," Medicine Crow remembered, "we discovered a network of trenches higher than your head and about three or four feet wide, going every which way. We took the main trench and followed it to the top of the hill, but it was tough going. The path was kind of steep, slushy, and muddy."

By the time Medicine Crow got to the top, about 30 or 40 soldiers who had gone before him had made the ground even more slippery. "To make matters worse," Medicine Crow said, "the guy in front of me was a fat, clumsy kid. He was always slipping and falling. When we finally reached the crest of the hill, he couldn't make it over the top. He'd get there, almost to the top, then slide down. Finally, I managed to push him up and over. Just then, the Germans opened fire, and he came sliding back down again and landed on top of me. I think that is the only

reason I didn't get killed myself that day. All the guys who had gotten on top were wiped out."

The next day the division was ordered to blow up the German bunkers. "As luck would have it," Medicine Crow said, "I was standing next to the commanding officer when the message came over the telephone. . . . The CO said, 'Well, Chief'—he always called me chief—'I guess if anybody can get through, you can. Get six men and go up there.'"

Before he could ask for volunteers, Medicine Crow recalled, "my closest buddy stepped up and said, 'Let's go, Chief.' In all, six guys, my closest friends, went with me. I was glad only six came forward because that made seven of us, and seven is one of the numbers considered lucky by Indians."

Before the soldiers left, the company commander ordered a smoke screen. "We can't afford to let these guys go in plain sight," he said, so guns from the American side began throwing smoke screen shells on the hill to give them cover, and soon the hillside was covered with a mass of white smoke. "Then," said Medicine Crow, "we took off. We didn't know where the mines were. We just took off. Meanwhile, the Germans realized something was happening, so they began lobbing mortar shells on us, here and there. We made it, but it took a long time crawling up that hill. It was slippery with wet snow and steep, but at least we did not set off any of the land mines."

Having arrived at the French side, the soldiers were given hot soup and coffee, and after resting briefly they were told to take off again. "They gave us boxes of dynamite with fuses," Medicine Crow said. "Each box weighed 50 pounds. We tried putting them on our shoulders, but the edges cut into our shoulders, and we couldn't walk down the hill carrying them in both hands. They were just too clumsy to handle. I didn't know what to do at first. Then I just sat down, set my box on my knees, and started sliding down the hill. The other guys saw me and did the same thing. Here we were, sliding behind one another down that hill. It wasn't fast, but we made it." Meanwhile, other soldiers had thrown smoke shells on the hillside to keep it foggy, but the Germans were lobbing mortar shells and hand grenades. Medicine Crow recalled, "If our boxes had gotten hit or if we had stepped on a mine, we would have been goners. It was a terrifying experience, but somehow we all came back without a scratch and with seven boxes of dynamite. The engineers then went ahead and blew up two or three of those big bunkers."

When Medicine Crow later told this story to the elders, they told him it was the same as leading a war party. Although he hadn't come back with horses or scalps, he had returned with materials essential to the welfare of his men. "That," he said, "was my first war deed."

Medicine Crow's next war deed was counting coup on a German soldier. After enjoying leave in France, he and his unit went back into Germany. Soon after crossing the border they came to a little town, which they were ordered to enter from the rear, while other units attacked it straight on. Despite the fact that it was March, said Medicine Crow, "There was still snow on the ground. To approach the town we had to wade through a slough up to our chests. I tell you it was wet and it was cold, but it was the safest way to get into town because the Germans had planted land mines all over."

Medicine Crow and the soldiers assigned to him were told to secure a back alley in the town. With his platoon behind him, Medicine Crow began running down the alley, which, despite gunfire in the main street, was quiet. "I was carrying an M1 rifle," he said:

Along one side of the alley was a stone wall about ten feet high. As I was running, I could see a gate, so I headed for it. I wanted to see what was happening on the main street. It turned out a German soldier had the same idea. He was running toward the gate, too, but from the other side of the wall. With all the shooting going on, I could not hear him and he could not hear me either. We met at the gate. My reactions were a bit quicker than his, and I was pretty spry in those days. I hit him under the chin with the butt of my rifle and knocked him down and sent his rifle flying. He landed on his back. He tried to reach for his rifle, but I kicked it out of the way. I dropped my rifle and jumped on top of him. As I sat on his chest, I grabbed his throat and started choking him. Meanwhile, the rest of my guys caught up. They wanted to shoot the German, but I still had my hands around his throat. He was scared. He began hollering, "Hitler Kaput! Hitler Kaput! Hitler nicht gude." He was crying. Tears were running down his face. I felt so sorry for him, I let him go.

Capturing the German counted as two war deeds. By knocking him down and touching him, Medicine Crow had counted coup on him, and he had also taken his weapon away from him, which was another coup.

The only coup that eluded Medicine Crow was also the most important: capturing a horse. The war was almost over before he managed it. "We were following a group of SS officers on horseback, about 50 of them," he explained. The

Pvt. Henry Bobb, a Paiute, operates direction-finding equipment for the 211th Coast Artillery at Momote Airstrip on Los Negros Island in the Admiralty Islands in 1944.

officers had abandoned their men, who surrendered by the thousands. Medicine Crow and his men followed the officers all night. "They were riding their horses on an asphalt road," he said, "and we could hear the clop, clop of the hooves ahead of us. About midnight, the horsemen left the highway and went to a farm about three miles down a dirt road. We followed their trail in the moonlight and arrived at a villa with a barn and a little fenced pasture."

As the commanding officer sat down with the platoon leaders to discuss how best to handle the situation, all Medicine Crow could think about, he said, were the horses in the corral. Having decided to attack the farmhouse at daybreak, the CO started telling the platoon leaders where to take their men. Medicine spoke up, saying, "Sir, maybe I should get those horses out of the corral before you attack, because some of those SS guys might be able to escape on them. It would only take me about five minutes." The

CO, he recalled, gave him a funny look, but all he said was, "OK, Chief, you're on." That was all Medicine Crow needed. As he described it,

I took one of my buddies, and we began sneaking down toward the corral and the barn. We had to be careful in case a German was in the barn on guard duty, watching. When we got there, nothing was moving. The horses were tired, just standing around. I crawled through the corral fence and came up to one of them. I said, "Whoa. Whoa," in English. He snorted a little bit, but he quickly settled down. I had this rope with me that I used to tie my blanket. I took that rope and tied his lower jaw with a double half hitch, just like the old-time Crow warriors used to do, and then I tried to get on. But it was a tall horse, and my boots were so muddy and caked up, I had a hard time mounting. Finally, I led the horse to the watering trough and stood on that to get on its back.

Medicine Crow had told his buddy that he was going to the other end of the paddock behind the horses, and as soon as he got there he would whistle, at which point the other soldier was supposed to open the gate and get out of the way. But as Medicine Crow recalled, "I got back there and whistled. Then I gave a Crow war cry, and those horses took off. There were woods about half a mile away, so I headed that way. Just about that time our boys opened fire on the farmhouse. By now it was coming daylight and I could get a good look at my horses. I had about 40 or 50 head. I was riding a sorrel with a blaze, a real nice horse. When we reached the woods and the horses started to mill around, I did something spontaneous. I sang a Crow praise song and rode around the horses. They all just looked at me."

The Germans had surrendered quickly and the firing was over, so Medicine Crow left the horses in the woods—except the one he was riding—and headed back to the farmhouse.

After the American soldiers had finished mopping things up and sending the prisoners to the rear, they departed down a gravel railbed. Medicine Crow, however, was still on the horse he had captured. "It was better to ride than walk," he said. "I felt good. I was a Crow warrior. My grandfathers would have been proud of me, I thought. But all too soon, the reality of the war came back. After letting me ride the horse for about a mile or so, the CO yelled over to me, 'Chief, you better get off. You make too good a target.'"

A SURVIVOR'S TALE

For some Native American soldiers, their memories of World War II are not of combat exploits but of simple survival. One of those soldiers was Alexander Mathews, a full-blood Pawnee from Oklahoma. The 88-year-old veteran, who died in 2008, is believed to have been the first Pawnee to see hostile action in World War II, on December 8, 1941, the day after the Japanese attack on Pearl Harbor. Taken prisoner in 1942, Mathews survived Japanese imprisonment to be released at war's end in 1945. Until his death he was also one of the two tribal members for whom the Pawnee Prisoner of War Song could still be sung. The honor now rests with the one remaining survivor, Gary Gover, who was captured in Vietnam.

In December 1941 Mathews (the surname was given to the family by a government interpreter who could not translate his father's actual name—Buffalo Chief) was with the 200th Coastal Artillery in the Philippines on the Bataan Peninsula, across a wide bay from Manila.

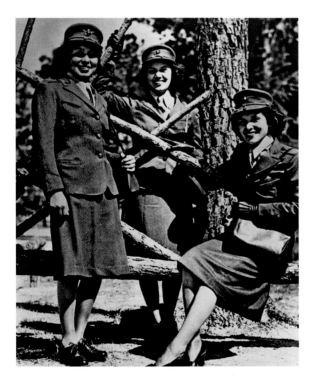

Three Native American women serving as Marine Corps reservists pose at Camp Lejeune, North Carolina, in 1943.

Their assignment was to shoot down Japanese aircraft attacking the fortified island of Corregidor. It was a hopeless task because the Japanese planes flew too high and fast for their 3-inch guns. His gun crew could claim to have shot down only one Japanese dive bomber before the ill-equipped and undersupplied forces on Bataan surrendered the following April.

As many as 70,000 Americans and their Filipino allies were then herded together for a forced march of some 70 miles to the first of many prison camps that would become their homes over the next four years. The prisoners, all of them hungry from insufficient rations and many already sick with malaria, dysentery, or other diseases, received little mercy from their Japanese captors, who considered them cowards for having surrendered. Those who lagged on the march were clubbed, bayoneted, and even shot. "I think the Japanese intent," Mathews said, "was for as many of us to die along the way as possible so that they wouldn't have to take care of us."

Mathews, who had attended the Haskell Institute before the war began, credited the discipline he had received at Indian school for helping him survive during his grueling 42 months as a prisoner of war.

"At Indian school we learned how to endure tough discipline. That experience was quite valuable in the sense that at that time Indian school was very military oriented," he recalled. During the Bataan Death March, Mathews met Phillip Coon, a Creek schoolmate from his days at Haskell. Coon survived the march, but another American Indian on Bataan, a Navajo named Herbert Sherman, did not. "Coon and I stuck together all the way through, even on work details, and today he's one of the few people I can talk to who even begins to understand the horrors of World War II in the Philippines," Mathews said

WWII hero Alexander Mathews in ceremonial dress retires the American flag shortly before his death in 2008.

shortly before his death. Of the 1,800 soldiers in his regiment, only 900 survived the war.

At war's end Mathews was in Japan unloading ships. "We figured the Yanks must be pretty close, the way our Jap guards were getting so fidgety. One morning we went to the docks to unload. It was quiet down where I worked. The Japanese, all in uniform, were listening to a radio. It was kind of easy, laying around. Finally, they came back and said, 'Yasame,' which means 'rest,' so we marched back to our area where we were staying. That's how I found out that we had dropped the atomic bombs way down on Hiroshima and Nagasaki. We were up north, and they hit down south. In a day or so, the guards came in and said they had surrendered."

During his captivity Mathews kept a diary made from rice paper. The August 15, 1945, entry reads, "Free at Last! WOW!"

JOSEPH MEDICINE CROW'S STORY

In his memoir *Counting Coup,* Joseph Medicine Crow describes the warrior tradition and his own response to being inducted into the Army in 1942: "In the pre-reservation days," he said, "a Crow young man aspiring to be a warrior would go into the Wolf Teeth Mountains seeking spiritual power. He believed that this power would make him a better warrior."

This experience, called "Going Without Water," was a three- or four-day total fast that was thought to encourage the appearance of emissaries of the Great Spirit. The animal spirits would ensure the vision seeker's success in battle. Some warriors added to the discomfort of the ritual by cutting off a finger. An alternative to seeking a vision was to be blessed by a veteran warrior or spiritual leader.

Medicine Crow opted not to undergo the ritual before shipping out, saying, "I preferred to do my communicating with the First Maker in church." But he did bring traditional "medicine" with him: a special feather he received from his uncle, Tom Yellowtail. Before each battle, Medicine Crow put the feather inside his helmet, recited prayers, and painted himself with a red lightning streak and red ring. "I did not put the paint on my face," he said, "but on my arms under my shirt. My uncle taught me how to paint myself properly. If I did not have paint, I could use a red pencil." It was this medicine, he says, that protected him despite a number of close encounters he had with the Germans.

On one occasion, Medicine Crow's company was marching when they came under artillery and mortar fire from Germans directly across a narrow valley. Despite the vulnerability of their position, Medicine Crow said, "I felt pretty well prepared. My haversack was full of pemmican my mother had sent me. I had my rifle. I had painted the symbols on my arms, and I had put the medicine feather in my helmet."

An artillery shell, though, soon exploded in front of Medicine Crow; the force knocked him over the side of a hill. Although he received only some bruises, he said, "It killed or wounded about a half dozen of the soldiers nearest me." His helmet, haversack, and rifle gone, Medicine Crow began the laborious task of ascending the hill. Along the way he found his rifle and then located his haversack.

"Near the last tree at the top of the hill," he remembered, "I found my helmet with the feather still tucked in the liner. When I put the helmet back on, I came to my senses. Everything was now all right, but I admit I had panicked there for a while. I have always attributed that particular sequence of good luck to my special Indian medicine. Whenever I had a close call, I would think about that medicine," Medicine Crow said.

During the war he relied on the medicine to accomplish four coups, or war deeds, against the Germans, earning his standing as a chief. Later he was awarded the Bronze Star and the French Legion of Honor Medal for his courage.

After he returned to the United States, Medicine Crow gave the feather to a fellow soldier, his cousin Henry Old Coyote, who was a machine gunner on a B-25 fighting in the European theater and Africa.

"I think after the Second World War that feather then went to Korea with a Crow soldier," Medicine Crow said. "It might have even gone to Vietnam. I don't know where it is now, but it certainly was powerful."

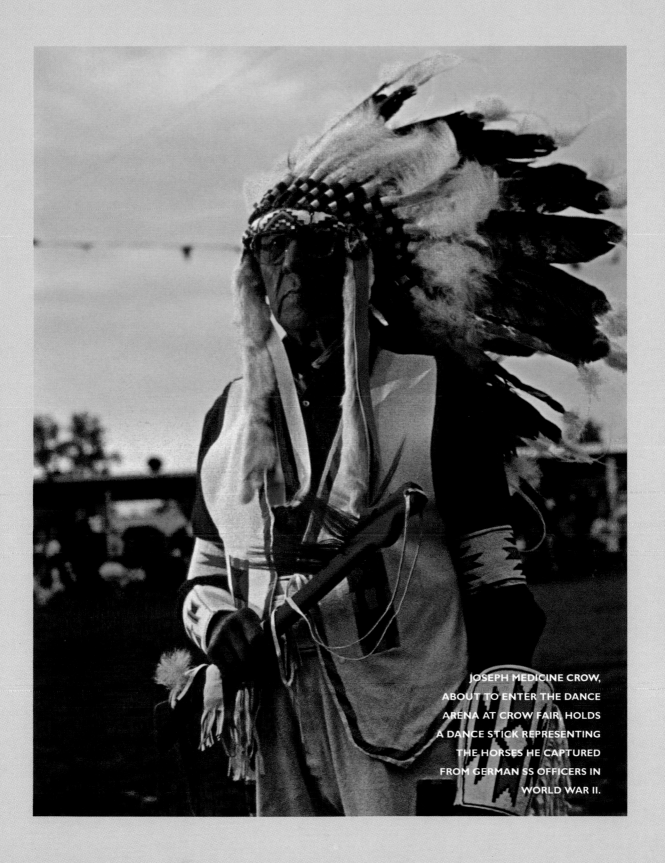

JOSEPH MEDICINE CROW, ABOUT TO ENTER THE DANCE ARENA AT CROW FAIR, HOLDS A DANCE STICK REPRESENTING THE HORSES HE CAPTURED FROM GERMAN SS OFFICERS IN WORLD WAR II.

BILL MAULDIN

One of the icons of World War II was the cartoonist Bill Mauldin, who served in the famed 45th Infantry Division. He served as an infantryman from 1941 through the end of the fighting in Sicily, where he was wounded. Mauldin's panels, published from 1940 to 1945 by military newspapers, featured two scruffy GIs known as Willie and Joe often making irreverent comments about their role in the war effort. As Mauldin later said, "I drew pictures for and about the soldiers because I knew what their life was like and understood their gripes." Willie and Joe at first sported 45th Division shoulder patches, but after Mauldin began drawing cartoons for the whole Army he omitted their sleeve insignias.

GIs loved his cartoons, and they were popular with most Americans back home, but Gen. George Patton regarded them as "scurrilous attempts to undermine military discipline" and threatened to have the military paper *Stars and Stripes* banned from his Third Army unless it dropped them. Gen. Dwight D. Eisenhower, Patton's boss, disagreed, and Mauldin continued to illustrate the humorous situations that came up.

Few fans of the cartoons, however, knew that Willie was based on Rayson Billey, a Choctaw Indian from Keota, Oklahoma. Billey was Mauldin's platoon sergeant. They became close friends. In the cartoons, Willie had a hooked nose and was the senior GI. Mauldin said, "I was Joe, the guy with the round face, sort of his straight man."

Mauldin said that Sergeant Billey taught him everything from rolling a pack to smarting off to officers without getting into trouble. "He was a tough, seasoned old soldier. And a decent man, a man who killed because it was what he had to do, not because he wanted to. He had lots of sides to him, this guy. He was my guru."

After being wounded, Mauldin was detached to the staff of *Stars and Stripes* but remained on the rolls of the 45th through war's end. In his 1969 book *The Brass Ring,* Mauldin wrote that he found his buddy lying dead on a battlefield in Sicily. "I saw him laying there bleeding from a lot of holes." Years later, when he attended the opening of the 45th Infantry Division Museum in Oklahoma City—"the only division reunion I ever went to"—Mauldin said, there was Rayson Billey.

"Where have you been?" Mauldin asked. "You're dead."

"I know," Rayson replied. "I read your book."

CLASSIC WILLIE AND JOE
GIs Willie and Joe, opposite, warm their hands from a tank's exhaust as they slog through snow.

STAR SPANGLED BANTER
Mauldin's early cartoon, above, from the *45th Division News*, makes light of GI life at Camp Barkeley, before the men were shipped overseas.

IN THE TRENCHES
In pelting rain, right, a miserable Joe wonders how many blankets his blissful buddy Willie has.

A BUGLER PLAYS TAPS DURING A
MEMORIAL SERVICE AT THE FIRST
MARINE CEMETERY IN HUNGNAM,
KOREA, FOR CASUALTIES OF THE
FIGHTING IN 1950 AT CHOSIN.

Chapter Five

FIGHTING THE SHORT WOLF MEN: KOREA

MEN OF THE FIRST MARINE
DIVISION ADVANCE
THROUGH THICK SMOKE
ALONG THE KOREAN
FRONT IN 1951.

Immediately following World War II and the Berlin airlift of food and supplies to that conquered city in 1947-48, another war began—the Cold War. The geopolitical chess match between Russia and the United States dominated the second half of the 20th century.

The Cold War had its hot moments, notably in Korea and Vietnam (see Chapter 6), where the United States sought to prevent the anticipated expansion of communism in Southeast Asia.

Overshadowed by World War II and Vietnam, the Korean War is often referred to as the forgotten war. It began June 25, 1950, when North Korean troops crossed the 38th parallel dividing the Korean Peninsula. It featured some of the most vicious fighting and worst conditions that American soldiers had ever experienced.

But it also was marked by remarkable accomplishments, from the morale-boosting landings at Inchon and the entrapment and remarkable escape of the First Marine Division at the Chosin Reservoir to the savage hill fighting at war's end. Three years of intense fighting had caused the combat deaths of almost 37,000 Americas.

Although China—which had supplied its neighbor North Korea with supplies, ammunition, and other support—the United States, and the United Nations agreed to an armistice in 1953, South Korea refused to sign, leaving the two Koreas separate and the war in suspension to this day.

America's native peoples paid scant heed to the geopolitical implications of the Cold War. Their country needed fighting men, and they answered the call. It was no matter that their adversaries now were the "Short Wolf Men" of Asia instead of the "Metal Hats" of Germany, the warriors in uniform again enlisted in numbers that far exceeded their percentage of the American population. Exact figures are difficult to establish, but it is believed that 10,000 Indians served in Korea and that, of the 54,000 American fatalities reported by the Department of Defense, 194 were Indians.

One of the American Indians who served in the Korean conflict was Ben Nighthorse Campbell, a Northern Cheyenne who later became one of the few American Indians ever to serve in the U.S. Congress. A high school dropout, Campbell joined the Air Force in 1951 and spent a year in a police unit in Korea.

Like other warriors in uniform, he greatly valued his military experience. "There was a camaraderie that transcends ethnicity when you serve your country overseas in wartime," he said in the Native American newsletter *Canku Ota* (Many Paths). After the war, Campbell devoted his life to judo and to politics, retiring in 2004 after serving three terms as a member of the U.S. House of Representatives and then two terms as a U.S. Senator from Colorado.

Another Native serviceman who achieved renown was Joseph J. "Jocko" Clark. Born in Pryor Indian Territory (later Oklahoma) to a Cherokee father, Clark attended the U.S. Naval Academy in Annapolis, Maryland, and was its first Native graduate.

With the outbreak of World War I, a newly graduated Clark served aboard an armored cruiser on combat duty in the Atlantic. He went

President Harry S. Truman presents Capt. Raymond Harvey (second from left) with the Medal of Honor. Harvey, a Chickasaw, was one of four Native Americans to be so honored during Korea.

on to serve in World War II and Korea, where he would become commander of the Seventh Fleet, before retiring as a full admiral.

Also an accomplished pilot, Clark drew on his heritage in naming the Cherokee Strike, a combat maneuver he devised that aided ground forces in Korea.

MEDALS OF HONOR

Four American Indians were awarded the Medal of Honor for heroism in Korea. One was Pvt. 1st Class Charles George, a Cherokee from North Carolina who sacrificed his life by throwing himself on a hand grenade to protect his fellow soldiers.

Capt. Raymond Harvey, a Chickasaw, led his platoon against entrenched positions, personally killing several of the enemy with carbine fire and hand grenades and then, although wounded, refusing to be evacuated until his company's objective had been achieved.

The third Medal of Honor recipient was Cpl. Mitchell Red Cloud, Jr., a Winnebago from Wisconsin and a veteran of World War II. Corporal Red Cloud, a member of Company E, 24th Infantry, was on a ridge guarding his company's command post when he exchanged fire with enemy troops who had launched a surprise attack. Although severely wounded, Red Cloud braced himself against a tree and continued shooting, thereby enabling his company to consolidate its position and evacuate the wounded. Corporal Red Cloud received the Medal of Honor posthumously on July 2,

"When a Man Goes into Battle, He Expects to Kill or Be Killed and If He Dies He Will Live Forever."

1951. On the monument erected in his honor at Black River Falls, Wisconsin, is inscribed, "The son of a Winnebago chief and warriors who believe that when a man goes into battle, he expects to kill or be killed and if he dies he will live forever."

The award of a posthumous Medal of Honor to a fourth Native American hero of the Korean War was authorized by Congress in 2007. Known to his family and friends as "Woody" and to his fellow soldiers as "The Chief," Woodrow Wilson Keeble is only now receiving recognition for his remarkable exploits on the battlefield in World War II and Korea.

A member of the Wahpeton Sisseton Sioux tribe of North Dakota, Sergeant Keeble was awarded five Purple Hearts, two Bronze Stars, a Silver Star, and a Distinguished Service Cross. Twice his men recommended him for the Medal of Honor but no action was taken during his lifetime. U.S. senators from both North and South Dakota—both states claim Keeble as a native son because the Wahpeton Sisseton Reservation straddles the state boundaries—wrote the legislation authorizing the posthumous honor.

Orphaned at the age of nine, Keeble spent most of his youth at the Wahpeton Indian Boarding School in North Dakota and returned there after his military service.

An exceptional athlete, he was being recruited by the Chicago White Sox as a pitcher when he was called to service in World War II. He saw combat throughout the South Pacific with the North Dakota Army National Guard's 164th Infantry Regiment, and he had a well-earned reputation for taking care of his men. As one recalled, "The safest place to be was next to Woody." In fact, he received his first Purple Heart and first Bronze Star on Guadalcanal while attempting to rescue several fellow soldiers.

When the Korean War broke out, Keeble reenlisted. Asked why, he said, "Someone has to teach those kids how to fight." Keeble returned to service at the age of 34 as a master sergeant. And it was from the Korean War that he

Cpl. Mitchell Red Cloud, a Winnebago from Wisconsin, was awarded the Medal of Honor posthumously.

emerged as the most decorated military hero in North Dakota history. To his comrades in arms he demonstrated behavior "often seen in movies but seldom seen on the actual place of combat," as Sgt. Joe Sagami said in recommending that Keeble receive the Medal of Honor.

Keeble's defining moment came on October 20, 1951, during Operation Nomad, the last major U.S. offensive of the war, as his company battled Chinese communist troops near Kumsong. Two days earlier he had engaged the enemy in a firefight for which he would later receive the Silver Star. Now, although already wounded twice and suffering from a badly damaged knee, Keeble ignored requests from medics and his men to remain behind when his company was ordered to take a nearby hill. Not until they had nearly reached the top, however, did the soldiers realize that they had climbed into an inescapable trap with entrenched enemy troops directly above them. "They were throwing so many grenades at us," one of the trapped soldiers remembered, "it looked like a flock of blackbirds flying over."

Keeble took matters into his own hands. Armed only with an M-1 rifle and hand grenades, he crawled toward the enemy and waged a one-man war. Thanks to his pitching skill, he managed to destroy three machine gun bunkers with well-aimed hand grenades, killing nine Chinese and wounding the other crew members. Although hit multiple times during this assault, including a hit by a concussion grenade that stunned him momentarily, he attacked two trenches filled with enemy troops, killing seven before the rest ran away. On the back side of the entrenchments, his soldiers found a Chinese command post, which explained why the enemy had fought so fiercely. For this exploit, Keeble received the Distinguished Service Cross.

Although he had fragmentation wounds in his chest, both arms, both thighs, right calf, and right knee, Keeble refused evacuation because no replacements were available. He returned to duty even though his wounds were bleeding through his bandages, he was limping badly, and he was so weak he could hardly lift his rifle. Little wonder that there has been such a determined effort to get Sergeant Keeble the medal he so richly deserved.

Following his service in Korea, Keeble returned to the Wahpeton Indian School, where he held several positions until a series of strokes rendered him speechless and unable to work. Hard times forced him to pawn some of his medals. He died in 1982 at the age of 65 and is buried in Sisseton, South Dakota. "It's hard to believe he had the warrior-like capabilities because outside of a war setting, he was so likeable," said Kurt Blue Dog, one of his relatives, in an article in *Indian Country* about the congressional action.

THE WARRIOR TRADITION

Another of the unsung heroes of the Korean War is Vernon Tsoodle, a member of the Kiowa Nation. Now living near Meers, Oklahoma, with his wife of 58 years, the Marine Corps veteran served two tours in Korea and two in Vietnam before retiring in 1973 with the rank of master gunnery sergeant (E-9) after 30 years of military service, including his time with the National Guard. He was awarded the Bronze Star for heroism during the Korean War. Like so many of the Native Americans in the military today, he is descended from noted warriors, and his family has followed in that tradition. Including those who have married into the Tsoodle clan, the family can claim more than 30 men and women who have served in the armed forces

"They Were Throwing So Many Grenades at Us, It Looked Like a Flock of Blackbirds."

since World War II, including his two sons, a daughter, and three grandchildren.

In addition to being influenced by ancestors, Tsoodle was shaped by other forces. In 1937, at the age of six, he was taken to Riverside Indian School in Anadarko, Oklahoma, because his grandparents, who were raising him, could barely make ends meet. Their only income was from farming and some money they got from grazing rights.

"You hear a lot of negative things about Indian boarding schools," Tsoodle said, "but for me they were a blessing because I learned things such as discipline, which later served me

well in the Marine Corps. A famous Marine general once said, 'The difference between being afraid and being helplessly frightened is discipline.' That applies not only to the Marine Corps but to life itself. If you are afraid, that's fine. If you are disciplined, you can handle any situation."

From Riverside he went to Chilocco Indian School for high school. Chilocco had a National Guard unit, but it was empty because everyone had been sent overseas to fight in World War II, so Tsoodle enlisted in the Oklahoma National Guard at the age of 14. "My rifle seemed like it was taller than I was," he remembered. Five

Although twice recommended for the Medal of Honor, Master Sgt. Woodrow Wilson Keeble (far left), with members of the 24th Infantry Division near Kunsong, Korea, did not receive it in his lifetime.

VERNON TSOODLE'S STORY

I was born in the vicinity of Mountain View, Oklahoma, in 1931. Tsoodle (Red Teepee), my great-grandfather, was the father of Satanta (White Bear), the great Kiowa warrior, and Old Man Tsoodle, my grandfather. Satanta was a member of an elite society of Kiowa warriors called Kaseenkos. Only the top ten warriors of the tribe could be members. I have been told that if that society still existed, I would be considered a member because of my war record.

Among the Kiowa people, the war record is the most important determinant of status within the tribe. From the war record flow all the great rewards of Kiowa culture. Because of my warrior lineage, I am a member of the Kiowa Gourd Clan. Its members were always the strongest and most able-bodied men of the tribe. It was their duty to protect the tribe and serve as hunters, warriors, and camp policemen.

I lived with my grandparents, Old Man Tsoodle and his wife, Kau Tompa Hodle. She was named after a skirmish at a swimming hole during which someone was killed. It was customary to give grandparents a child to raise since they had no more children of their own at home and the grandchild would be around to help take care of them. It was also a way to ensure that tribal traditions and culture would be carried on by the next generation.

Since my grandparents could not speak English, I learned to speak Kiowa. That enabled me to converse with other elders. That was one of the advantages of being raised by your grandparents because you got exposed to other elders within the tribe.

As a child, I heard many stories about Kiowa warriors from the tribal elders who visited my grandparents. For example, I learned that when our horsemen would close in on their enemies, the war chiefs would shout, *"Bay-Pae-Tay! Bay-Pae-Tay!"* "Courage! Courage!" Whenever I was engaged with the enemy during my tours in Korea and Vietnam, those words would race through my mind.

When WWII broke out all of my siblings enlisted almost instantly. My brother Fred joined the Army Air Corps and my brothers Hawley and Brennen and my sister Mildred joined the Navy. Their example inspired my brother Thee and me to pursue careers in the military.

My grandfather was a keeper of one of the sacred bundles of the Kiowa tribe, the Ten Grandmothers bundle. Every day during the war he took out that bundle and prayed. He prayed not only for his grandchildren but also for all the other members of the Kiowa tribe who were in the military and for our country's success in the war.

My grandmother was also very patriotic, but I don't think she fully understood what was happening. She would express her patriotism whenever an airplane flew over our homestead. It didn't matter what kind of plane it was—a military plane or a commercial airliner, like Braniff or TWA. As soon as she saw the plane she would stop whatever she was doing and give a loud trill called a lulu, which is a cry a Kiowa woman makes when she is proud and happy. She did it to show her pride, knowing that her grandkids were defending our country and our people.

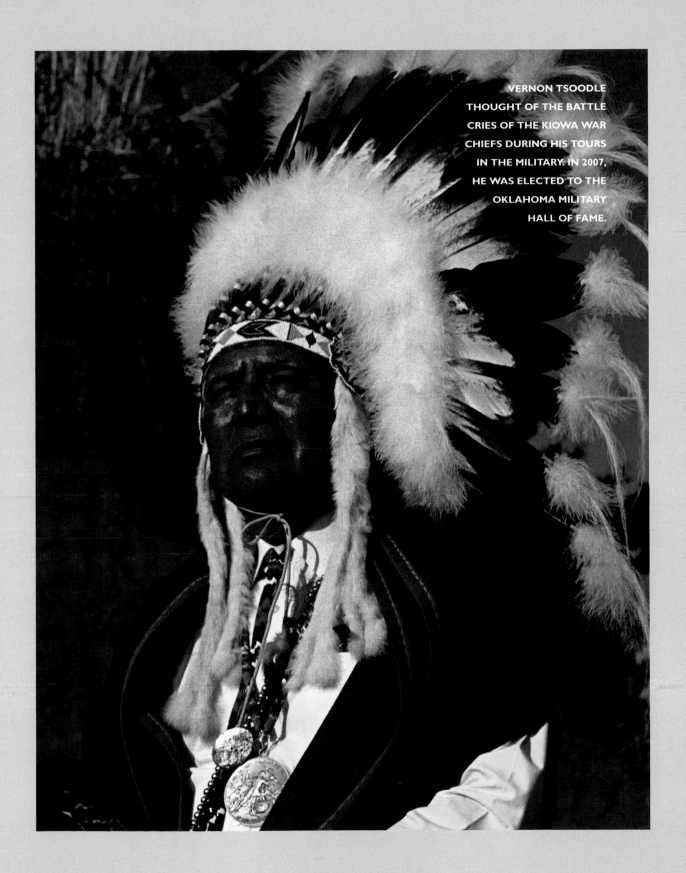

VERNON TSOODLE
THOUGHT OF THE BATTLE
CRIES OF THE KIOWA WAR
CHIEFS DURING HIS TOURS
IN THE MILITARY. IN 2007,
HE WAS ELECTED TO THE
OKLAHOMA MILITARY
HALL OF FAME.

FIGHTING THE SHORT WOLF MEN: KOREA

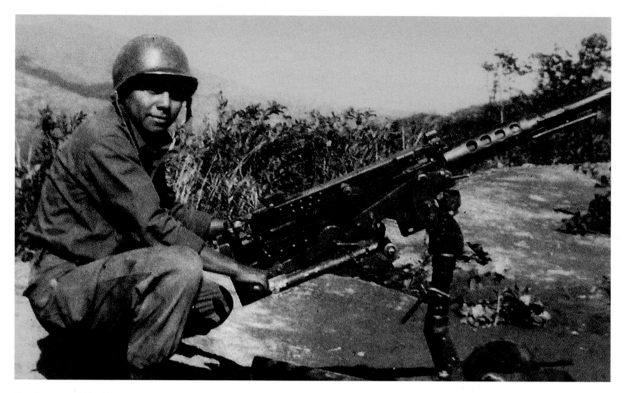

Sgt. Raymond Wahkinney, a Comanche who operated a 105-mm howitzer, saw some of the bloodiest fighting of the Korean war at places like Pork Chop Hill, Old Baldy, and Heartbreak Ridge.

years later he married a high school classmate, Jimmie Leah Reese. With the return of veterans from World War II, Tsoodle couldn't find a job, so he enlisted in the Marine Corps. "I had to keep my marriage a secret, however," he said, "because the Marine Corps was not accepting anyone who was married."

The discipline Tsoodle received at Riverside and Chilocco inured him to the rigors of boot camp. "At Indian boarding school," he said, "we were taught when to eat, when to brush our teeth, when to breathe. Boot camp was a snap compared to Indian schools."

After graduating from boot camp, in response to the worsening situation in Korea, Tsoodle was rushed to the peninsula. Years later he still remembered a magnificent display of firefighting over the city of Inchon when he first arrived.

In Korea Tsoodle was a communications lineman, ensuring landline communications between each unit, because radios were not always reliable. This often put him in hostile territory stringing wires. He recalled sitting at the top of a telephone pole connecting a wire when fighting broke out in a village about a half mile away. "I was mesmerized watching the firefight and Marines moving from door to door through the town," he said. "I watched for what seemed like a long time until it dawned on me that I was a sitting duck on top of that pole and that a sniper could take me down in one second. You never saw someone scurry down a pole as quick as I did that night!"

Tsoodle wound up with the Marines trapped at the Chosin Reservoir, where some 16,000 U.S. servicemen—including 12,000 Marines—

faced more than 100,000 Chinese soldiers. The Chosin campaign prompted the famous Marine cry "Retreat, hell. We're attacking in a different direction."

The soldiers earned the nickname "Frozen Chosin." Tsoodle said the cold was no exaggeration:

We did not realize how cold it was until we got up there. Temperatures of 30 and 40 degrees below zero were common. The ground was so frozen we couldn't dig foxholes. We had to lay behind rice paddy dikes and things like that for protection. You couldn't build a fire because you would give your position away. All you could do was just lay there and endure the cold. I remember being served a wonderful Thanksgiving dinner with all the fixings but it froze solid while I was eating it. Even had there been no enemy shooting at us, we wondered how we could survive.

Having been cut off by the Chinese, members of the wire team were faced with the grim job of unloading the wounded and the dead from incoming helicopters. "Many of the dead that we unloaded were in grotesque positions," Tsoodle remembered, "because once they were killed, they froze in that position. If we saw steam coming from their noses, we knew they were still alive and we carried them over to the medics so they could triage them by determining which men would live and which men wouldn't. It was a sorrowful job but you had to do it."

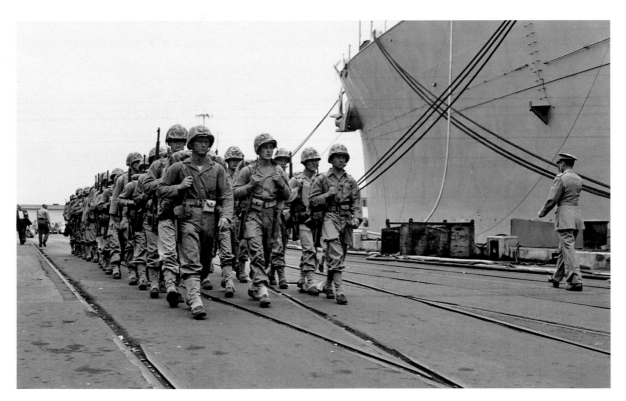

Men from the First Marine Division march down a pier to board the U.S.S. *Henrico,* an attack transport that participated in the historic landing at Inchon, Korea, in 1950.

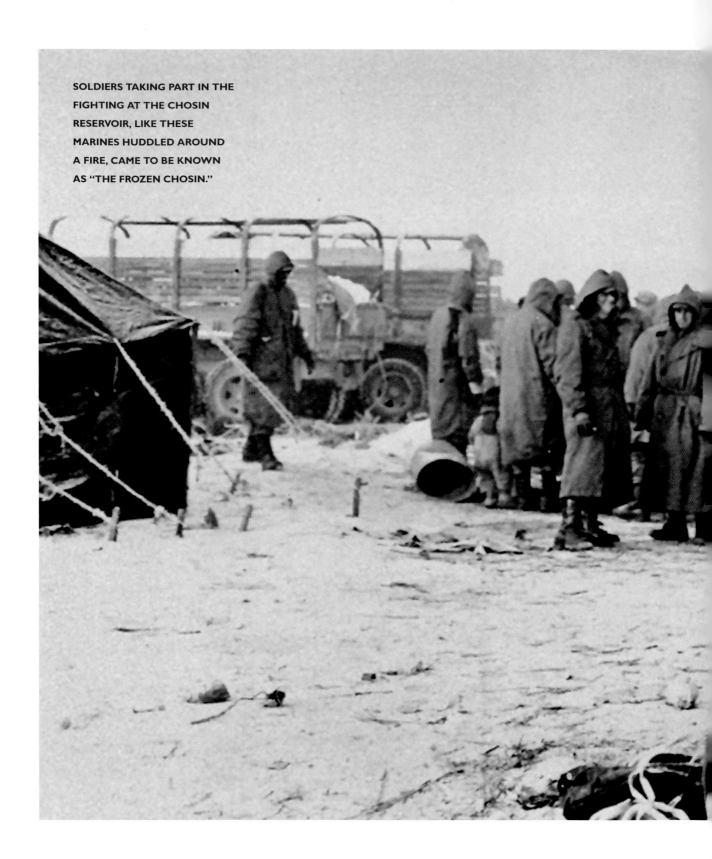

SOLDIERS TAKING PART IN THE
FIGHTING AT THE CHOSIN
RESERVOIR, LIKE THESE
MARINES HUDDLED AROUND
A FIRE, CAME TO BE KNOWN
AS "THE FROZEN CHOSIN."

WARRIORS IN UNIFORM

"If You Shot Out There, You Were Going to Hit Somebody and Sure as Heck, We Did."

Tsoodle saw frontline action when the First Marine Division was ordered to the village of Hagaru-ri to set up division headquarters. On the east side of Hagaru-ri was a vital airstrip. Tsoodle, with the First Signal Battalion, was part of the advance party to tie headquarters to the Fifth and Seventh Marine Regiments, which were set up north and west of Hagaru-ri at the end of the Chosin Reservoir.

Upon leaving division headquarters they began stringing their lines overhead so track vehicles like tanks wouldn't tear them up, but just as they got to the edge of the headquarters compound, they started receiving sniper fire. Not knowing what was going on, they called the division wire officer, who ordered them to come back. Only then did they realize that they were surrounded.

With the Chinese now pressing them on all sides, Marines not assigned specific duties were formed into rifle platoons. Tsoodle's military specialty was telephone communications, but he had first been trained by the Marines to be an infantryman, he says, "so in situations such as this, they can take you and put you on a piece of equipment such as a machine gun, and you shouldn't have any problem operating it." The wire team was turned into a .30-caliber machine gun squad and tasked with defending the airstrip.

To reach their defensive position, they had to go up a steep incline to reach the ridgeline. "We had to re-supply ourselves with ammunition, which meant carrying M-1 bandoliers and grenades," Tsoodle said. The icy terrain made maneuvering in their winter boots difficult for the soldiers.

When it was Tsoodle's turn to make the trip, he strapped on six bandoliers of ammunition and started up the hill. "I'd make a little headway and then start losing traction, so I'd take off a bandolier to lighten the load," he said. "I'd make a little more headway and slip again so I'd have to lose another bandolier. By the time I made it to the top, I was wearing only one bandolier! The next Marine in line tried to do the same thing, with the same results."

On the opposite hill, Tsoodle noticed a number of brown spots—foxholes that were dug by the Chinese. The soldiers set up their machine guns behind a rice paddy revetment and waited for the Chinese to attack.

The attack came at night. "We always knew when [the Chinese] were coming," Tsoodle said, "because they would start yelling and screaming and shooting off tracers. I can still remember the bells and whistles that signaled the Chinese to attack. The Chinese would come running down the hill with all kinds of noise makers, and they would fill the air with green incendiary or tracer rounds that ricocheted off the rice paddies all around us because the ground was so frozen."

As fighting continued, the machine gun barrels got red hot and the soldiers fired aimlessly. "You didn't even have to pick out a target," Tsoodle said, "because if you shot out there, you were going to hit somebody and sure as heck, we did. When daybreak arrived, it was nothing to see hundreds of Chinese lying dead out there."

One night the Chinese decided to attack the Americans' tank park, setting off 55-gallon

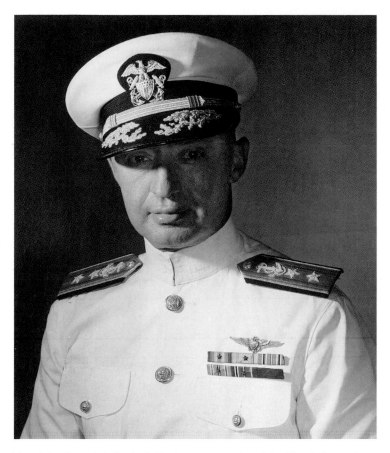

Vice Adm. Joseph J. "Jocko" Clark, a commander of the Navy's Seventh Fleet during the Korean War, was of Cherokee descent.

drums of diesel fuel. When the drums exploded, the entire sky was lit up, illuminating thousands of Chinese coming down from the hill. Tsoodle recalled that they looked like "ants whose hill had been disturbed." Because the crews slept around their tanks, they were able to react quickly and defend themselves. The next day, as they walked among the dead Chinese soldiers, the Americans could see that many of them carried only a blanket, tooth powder, a toothbrush, and a comb. Their food was grain strapped around their body, said Tsoodle, like a bandolier, and despite the extreme cold, they were wearing only tennis shoes and quilted cotton uniforms. "That was their cold weather gear," Tsoodle said.

"You sure had to pity them because they were in worse shape than we were."

The UN forces succeeded in getting out, but at a terrible cost; there were something like 10,000 casualties, many of them because of the intense cold.

Tsoodle was awarded the Bronze Star with the Combat V (next page) because he was in charge of the machine gun section, which held the Chinese away from the airfield. Despite having been a participant in one of the major battles of the conflict, Tsoodle said, "In situations like that you don't realize how much peril you are in until after it's over. I was just a gung-ho 18-year-old Marine doing his job."

An inscription on the Korean War monument in Washington, D.C., says, "All gave some, some gave all." Tsoodle, who considers himself "one of the lucky ones," grows emotional when he thinks of the Marines who did not make it out. "I think of them and then I wonder why, despite four combat tours—two in Korea and two in Vietnam—I never got a scratch."

And Tsoodle's luck extended to his family:

When I was getting ready to ship out of Korea, people at the debarkation port started telling me that there was a guy who looked just like me asking for me. I knew exactly who it was, my brother Thee. He was also with the Marines, and he had walked something like ten hours just to see me off. We spent my last night in Korea together and he watched me leave the next day. It was one of the hardest things

PRIVATE TSOODLE'S BRONZE STAR

The Bronze Star is awarded to "any person who … distinguished himself or herself by heroic or meritorious achievement or service … in connection with military operations against an armed enemy; or while engaged in military operations involving conflict with an opposing armed force in which the United States is not a belligerent party." The citation accompanying Tsoodle's bronze star reads as follows:

"For heroic achievement in connection with operations against an enemy while serving with a Marine signal company in Korea on 28 November 1950. Private First Class Tsoodle, acting as a machine gunner in a machine gun squad of a reinforced rifle platoon comprised of communications personnel, displayed

Pvt. 1st Class Vernon Tsoodle's Bronze Star had an attached V for valor because he displayed courage under fire while serving in Korea.

outstanding professional skill and initiative. When his platoon was assigned the mission of reinforcing an infantry company in defense of the Hagaru-ri, Korea, airstrip, he fearlessly assumed an exposed position and placed accurate and effective fire on enemy positions. Despite numerous casualties suffered by his platoon, he continued to remain in position throughout the night and, by his fire, inflicted numerous casualties on the enemy. His aggressive actions were an inspiration to all members of his platoon and contributed materially to the successful defense of the airstrip. Private First Class Tsoodle's initiative and courageous actions were in keeping with the highest traditions of the United States Naval Service."

"I Wonder Why, Despite Four Combat Tours…, I Never Got a Scratch."

I've ever had to do, leaving my brother behind and not knowing if we would ever see each other again. However, he served his time in Korea and came home safely. It was a joyous reunion when we saw each other again. We were the closest in age, so we had a special bond.

Tsoodle said that when he joined the Marines he never saw himself as an Indian:

I was a Marine. As a Marine you develop close ties with other Marines because you are together for extended periods of time, away from your homes and families and dependent on each other for survival. Our bond was common. We were no longer separated by race. We were Marines. Because I was an Indian, however, my fellow Marines throughout my career called me "Chief." People have often asked if that offended me. It didn't, and it still doesn't. It was never said or meant in a derogatory manner. To them a chief was a leader, so how could that be a bad thing to be compared to? I was pleased because a chief is a great warrior.

JOHN EMHOOLAH

Few families—either Indian or non-Indian—can rival the military record of the Emhoolah brothers. Six saw active duty. A seventh brother tried to enlist but failed the physical. John, Parker, and Farrell served in the Army; Lonnie, Hubert, and James were in the Marines. All but

Lonnie and Farrell saw combat either in Korea or Vietnam; all survived; and all graduated from college, even though they were raised in a traditional, Kiowa-speaking household—Farrell was born in a tepee. The family name, which means "Kills the Enemy" or "Man Killer," comes from the Arapaho side of the family.

John Emhoolah, the eldest of the brothers and the family spokesman, agreed to tell his story. His world, he said, changed the day an official of the Bureau of Indian Affairs drove out to the family homestead near Anadarko and took him away to boarding school.

"At Riverside Indian School they took away your culture, took away your language. They made it really tough on students. While there, I learned that if you joined the National Guard you got some money after every three months, so quite a few of us signed up and became members of the Oklahoma Thunderbird Division."

The year was 1950 and Emhoolah was a sophomore in high school. Almost immediately his unit was mobilized because of the Korean War. "There must have been 20 or 30 of us from Riverside Indian School," he recalled. "The majority of the 45th division—about 60 or 70 percent—were Native American, so I had a lot of friends and relatives among the other tribes—Comanche, Cheyenne, Arapaho, Kiowa. One of them was my cousin on the Arapaho side, Milney Dawes."

Emhoolah was assigned to the 158th Field Artillery as a forward observer. After training in Japan, he formed part of the landing force at Incheon, Korea, and then moved inland to

Kiowa John Emhoolah, the eldest of six brothers to serve in WWII, was a forward observer in the 158th Field Artillery.

what was known as the MLR, the main line of resistance, where his unit dug bunkers and settled in for the winter. From their bunkers, the American troops could see the Chinese digging their own trenches into the mountain across the way.

"We were up there from December through April. That's how long I was on the front lines," Emhoolah said. "We had no heat up there. I felt sorry for the infantry guys because they had even less warmth than we had. You couldn't light a fire. You could smoke; but you had to be out of sight."

One day, Emhoolah helped set up a field kitchen. As a gesture of thanks, the field cooks baked him a big sheet cake. "I knew I couldn't eat it by myself, and I thought about my cousin Milney, who was in a forward observation post about a hundred yards in front of the main line. He was with three other guys—one of them was a lieutenant."

"Now We Can Use Our Eagle Feathers. We Can Have Our Powwows. We Can Sing Our Songs."

The soldiers' job was to spot the enemy and report any movement in the surrounding area. To reach the outpost, Emhoolah had to crawl through a tunnel with all his gear.

"I had my weapons with me, and my back pack, and at the same time I'm taking that cake," he said. "I got real muddy, too, but those guys were so glad, so happy to see me, especially Milney. We ate that cake and we visited till evening time, when I said I had to get back to my unit."

Before Emhoolah left, Milney asked him to take his medicine bundle for safekeeping. "John," he said, "I don't feel good about this mission. I'm not going to make it."

Emhoolah said he tried to encourage him. "I told him, 'Sure, you'll make it. Be alert. Be alert at all times.' But I guess it was not to be, because that was the last time I saw him. They all must have fallen asleep, because during the night the enemy snuck in and cut their throats.

"While I was up on that mountain freezing, I did a lot of thinking." Emhoolah said. "I thought, 'We don't have that freedom of religion like all other people have. We can't celebrate or do our religious ceremonies like all the others: the Catholics, the Methodists, you name it. They get to do what they want. But not we Indians. We can't even use our eagle feathers.'"

Upon his return home, Emhoolah took up a career in Denver, with the American Indian Higher Education Consortium, and he lobbied for religious freedom. "I got lawyers involved," he said. "I said, 'Here's the problem: We Indians fought a war. We come back and we still got this suppression of Indian people. We need to find a way to make it possible for Indian people to have freedom of religion.'"

"Well," Emhoolah smiled, "word got around. To all different tribes. We started a movement. Congress passed, and Jimmy Carter signed, the Native American Indian Religious Freedom Act. Now we can use our eagle feathers. We can have our powwows. We can sing our songs."

And, thanks to the American Indian College Fund, Indian people now have access to higher education. "So, you see," said Emoolah, "it's all those things. When you go fight a war, you're not going over there just to kill, you're going over there to make life a little better when you come back. That's the way I looked at it."

ONE OF THE "CHOSIN FEW"

Another Native veteran of the Korean War is Gilbert Towner, a member of the Tututni, one of the Siletz Confederated Tribes of Oregon. One of the last speakers of the Tututni language, Towner is proud of his warrior legacy. His Indian name is Ensalun, the name of his great-grandfather, who was a war leader of the Tututni in the Rogue River Wars of Oregon. Family members of Towner's also served in World War I and II. Interviewed for the First Warrior Project, which has preserved the images and stories of 100 Indian veterans, Towner said, "We uphold the tradition of my great-grandfather. We are Americans."

Like his friend Vernon Tsoodle, he was one of the "Chosin Few." On the night of April 23, 1951, while in a foxhole atop a mountain ridgeline, Towner was shot in both legs and an arm. A

Sgt. First Class John Rice, a Winnebago, was denied burial in his native Sioux City, Iowa, but President Truman arranged for burial with full military honors at Arlington Cemetery.

fellow Marine hunkered down with him was in even worse shape. "He was losing a lot of blood," Towner said, "and could hardly raise his rifle to shoot. I figured that if he stayed there he would die from his wounds, so I decided to try to get him to the medics."

Towner crawled out of the foxhole thinking he would lift the wounded soldier out, but, unable to stand, managed instead to drag him out of the hole by using his belt to tie both of the soldier's hands together and slinging the soldier's arms over his head. The two had crawled out of the foxhole a short way when they encountered three Chinese who had broken through. "They were just sitting there, evidently exhausted or disoriented," Towner

said. "I shot all three of them with my pistol and then we continued on our way down the backside of the mountain to the aid station." Towner refused treatment himself and crawled back to his position, but suffering from wounds in both legs, his arms, and his head, he had to be carried off the mountain the next morning.

A sergeant who witnessed his heroics promised to recommend Towner for a Silver Star. He did get three Purple Hearts, but the Silver Star never came. "I was new to the outfit—I came up that night—and nobody knew me," Towner explained.

In many respects, life for him was worse after the war. Like so many soldiers, he never fully recovered physically or emotionally from the stress of combat. Unable to meet the Marine

"It Was Scary Being in Combat, but I Tried Not to Think Too Much About It."

physical requirements because of his injuries, Towner took his discharge in 1958. "I just went home and tried to pick up my life where I'd left off, but I couldn't do it," he said. "I had been a logger before I joined the Marine Corps and tried to go back to the same job, but I couldn't do the work because of the wounds. Also, because of things I went through, I used to have some real bad dreams. I was in real bad shape. I drank an awful lot. I tried to use alcohol to overcome my problems, but it didn't help." For eight years Towner wandered the streets, working when he could, before reconnecting with his Indian culture. "I relied heavily on my Indian culture, using the sweathouse, to straighten myself out," he said.

Towner eventually succeeded. He got married and found employment with the U.S. Postal Service, the first of a series of government jobs that would last for 25 years and enable him to earn disability retirement.

Today, he still lives with the pain of his wounds, and with their consequences. In winter, the skin on his hands cracks at the joints, and he is afflicted by degenerative arthritis—the result of the severe frostbite he suffered in Korea. And like others who shared such experiences, he still suffers from those memories. Nonetheless, he says he is now content. He has been married for 20 years, has four children and five adopted stepchildren, and he is an honored member of his tribe.

"I don't feel sorry for myself at all," he said. "I just thank God I'm alive and able to meet the new day."

His sentiments were echoed by Raymond "Rusty" Wahkinney, a Comanche who experienced some of the heaviest and bloodiest fighting of the war. Sergeant Wahkinney, a member of the Oklahoma National Guard who died in February 2007, also was haunted by his memories. He talked about a cold so intense that tanks could cross major rivers without breaking through the ice. He experienced combat so brutal it seemed no one would come home alive. He recalled sitting back to back with his buddy in their foxhole on the front lines during the nighttime attacks as bullets and shrapnel flew around them.

The youngsters in his command would break down and cry, sobbing that they would never see home again. "I would talk to them," he said. "I told them to pray because the Lord will take care of you. That would calm them down for a while, but then it would start all over again the next night. It was scary being in combat, but I tried not to think too much about it. I would concentrate on what I was supposed to be doing, and that was operating a 105-mm cannon."

During his three years in Korea with the 158th Field Artillery of the famed Thunderbird Division, Sergeant Wahkinney's unit fired 15,373 rounds at the North Korean and Chinese armies as they slugged it out at Pork Chop Hill, Old Baldy, Heartbreak Ridge, and the other bloody engagements that marked the Korean War. Like other Indian servicemen, he was called "Chief." "The nickname never bothered me," he said, "because I saw myself as a warrior fighting for all Indian people as well as for my country."

UNIFORMS

An indication of the pride Native Americans have in their veterans can be seen at parades and ceremonies on reservations and at public events near Indian communities. Women wear shawls that bear the names of military personnel and their units. Veterans wear cherished items of military apparel. Often these are embellished with beadwork, feathers, or other tribal identifiers. There is no better place to see this blending of Native American cultures and military pride than during the grand entry at powwows where veterans and active-duty personnel lead the assembled dancers into the arena carrying the American flag and their tribal flags.

Although the veterans and their families seldom wish to part with the medals, ribbons, and other military honors they earned from their country, a few of them are now making their way into museum collections like those shown here that are now in the custody of the National Museum of the American Indian in Washington, D.C.

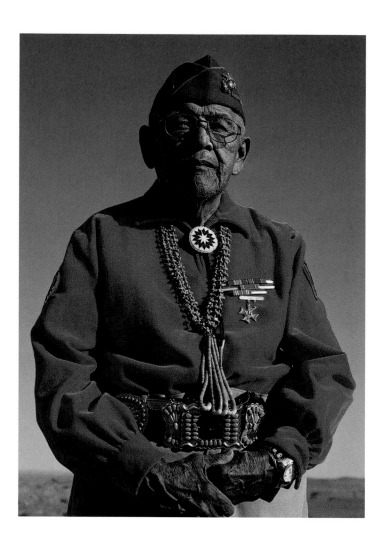

VETERAN DRESS
A U.S. Army WWII veteran wears an Army-issue field hat and several service pins, including the Distinguished Service Cross. These are embellished by a beaded necklace, tie, and belt.

FIELD HAT
This WWII-era hat includes logos for the VFW and the Montana American Legion.

DECORATED SHIRT

This U.S. Army shirt features sergeant stripes on the shoulders and a variety of service pins, including the WWII Victory Medal, the Bronze Star, the Asiatic Campaign Medal, marksmanship badges, and a beaded buckskin patch indicating the "All Indian Company"—Company B, 163rd Infantry, 41st Division.

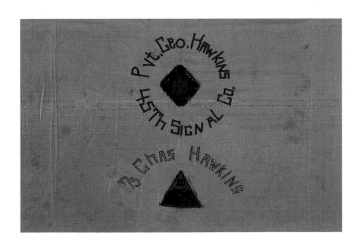

BEADED SHAWL

This detail from a shawl made by Katie Haag Hawkins during World War II features the beaded insignia of the 45th Infantry Division. In a circle around it is beaded Pvt. Geo. Hawkins and 45th Signal Co. Below it is another insignia, with the name Chas. Hawkins beaded above it.

U.S. MARINES REST
IN HUE AFTER A
BATTLE DURING
THE TET OFFENSIVE.

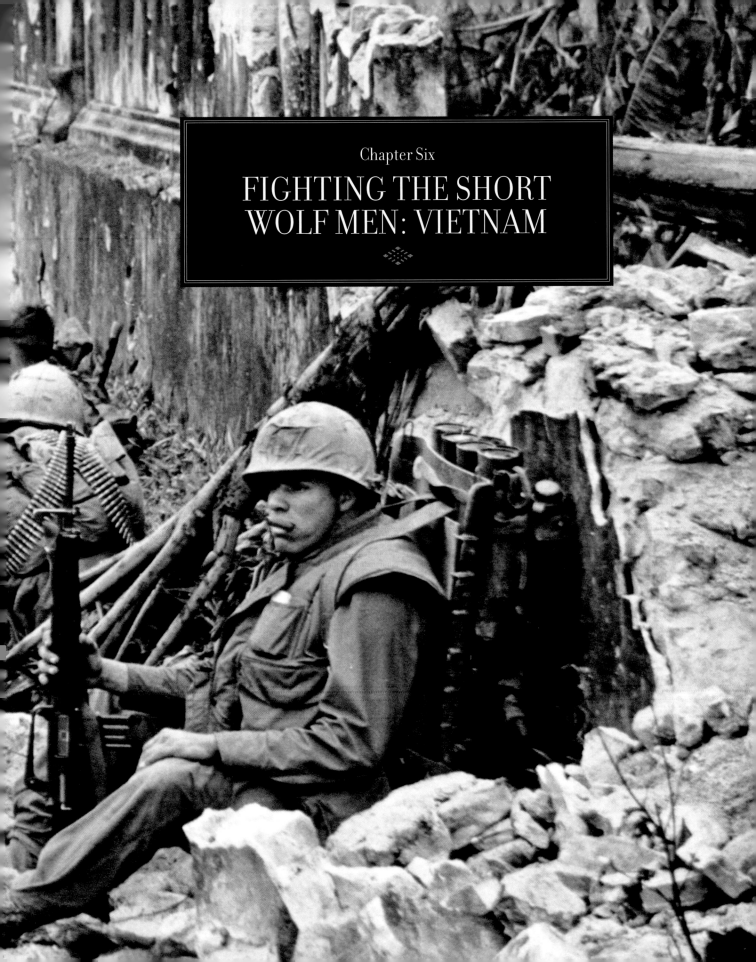

Chapter Six

FIGHTING THE SHORT
WOLF MEN: VIETNAM

AN AMERICAN GI, WEAPON DRAWN, CAUTIOUSLY MOVES OVER A DEVASTATED HILL NEAR FIREBASE GLADIATOR.

Of the more than 42,000 Indians who served in the military during the Vietnam era, 135 were members of the Crow Nation of Montana including Carson Walks Over Ice, a nephew of Joseph Medicine Crow (see Chapter 4). Like his uncle, Walks Over Ice had grown up hearing stories about great Crow warriors of the past, and he volunteered to go to Vietnam even though his service commitment was about to end, because he wanted to live up to the warrior traditions of his people.

Ernie Dogwolf Lovato, an Apache from Lingo, Wyoming, joined the Marines and went to Vietnam for the same reasons. In an account of his experience preserved by the American Native Press Archives and Sequoyah Research Center, Lavato expresses well the conflict inherent in trying to follow ancient traditions in the modern world. "The greatest thrill to a young man is to become a warrior and get status within the tribe," he says. "That's our ultimate goal. The sad thing about becoming a warrior these days, however, is that [the tribes]. . .are no longer counting coup. It's got to be a war. So, how do we get our young ones to be warriors without killing them? I [now] feel strongly. . . that being a warrior is really not as important as having a son or a daughter, and watching their sons give them children and grandchildren. There are a lot of men [who went to Vietnam] that will never know their grandchildren. I'm the fortunate one. I've got nine grandbabies."

Nonetheless, as is evident from Walks Over Ice's story, the warrior tradition provides a common bond, a shared brotherhood in the U.S. military, even with members of tribes that were traditional enemies: Walks Over Ice's best friend, and adopted brother, was Richard Spider, a Sioux, once the mortal enemies of the Crow.

SHARING A BOND

Although few in number, relatively speaking, Native American soldiers seek each other out, regardless of tribal affiliation. John Luke Flyinghorse, Sr., a Hunkpapa Lakota from McIntosh, South Dakota, another Vietnam veteran whose account is archived by the research center, tried to explain: "American Indians always looked each other up . . . no matter what tribe we were from. That was the only mystique. . . . Why? I have no idea, but we had a bond. . . . No matter where we came from, we always walked point, or carried the radio, or were the Company Commander's operator . . . always."

As Walks Over Ice points out, Indians were always expected to be a little bit better than their non-Indian companions. "We had a certain reputation to live up to," he says. Of course, not all Indian soldiers appreciate that pressure. In fact, many soldiers of American Indian heritage who grow up away from traditional communities and values are dismayed to find themselves thrust into dangerous situations because the fact that they are Indian supposedly makes them "super" soldiers.

Typical is the experience of the Vietnam veteran who told Tom Holm, author of *Strong Hearts, Wounded Souls,* that whenever his unit went on patrol, his lieutenant made him walk point, which meant he was in front of the patrol

"As I Went Down, I Could See the Muzzle Flashes from the Machine Gun."

looking out for ambushes and booby traps. Finally, the soldier asked his lieutenant, "Why are you doing this to me?" "Well, you're an Indian," the officer replied. "You know your way around the woods." "I was born and raised in Chicago," the soldier answered.

THE SPIRIT WORLD

One bond that most Native American soldiers share is a staunch belief in the spirit world. Religion is at the core of Native life. Rituals and sacred objects are closely held, with few non-Natives allowed access to the secrets of the kiva, the sweat lodge, or the Sun Dance.

The Sun Dance, which is the highest religious expression of the tribes of the northern plains including the Crow, is usually a three-day ceremony in which participants abstain from food and water while dancing and blowing a whistle made from a hollow eagle wing bone. Dancers often suffer under extremes of weather. Some collapse from hunger and exhaustion in their effort to communicate with the spirit world as they seek visions, help with personal problems, or blessings for friends and relatives.

Bobby Talks Different, a Vietnam veteran of the Gros Ventre tribe from the Fort Belknap Reservation in northern Montana, danced eight times. "I did this to keep my promise to the One Above, he says. "Eight of us . . . went to Vietnam together and I promised the One Above to do a Sun Dance for each life that returned. All eight of us came back, and I thanked the One Above by undergoing eight Sun Dances. The others never knew of my vow."

The story of Carson Walks Over Ice is not unique among Native American soldiers; what is unusual is his willingness to share it. When he went to Vietnam in 1966 he took into battle two medicines—one that he wore around his neck and one that he wore around his waist—and credits them for his courageous performance and his safe return home.

"I certainly had some close calls," he says, "like the day my platoon was directed to search an area recently burned clear by napalm. When about half of my platoon was across the burned out area, I was about to step out into the open when a voice right next to me says, 'Hey, there is something wrong. Watch out!' I looked around but nobody was there, so I stepped out. At once a machine gun to my right opened up. The ground around me literally exploded. As I went down, I could see the muzzle flashes from the machine gun. I began shooting. I killed the gunner; he fell backwards. Another guy stepped in; I shot him. Then a third guy came forward; I shot him. As he fell, I jumped up, and at that moment a bullet tore my wristwatch off, leaving a red mark across my arm, but I didn't realize it at the time." As Walks Over Ice moved away, another machine gun crew opened up on him, but again they missed. "I was able to cut around to the side and kill those gunners," he says, "but by then I was shaking because of the adrenaline rush. As I tried to calm down, I looked at my wrist to see the time, but there was no watch. Since then I can't wear a watch. I don't know why, but when I put a watch on my wrist, it stops."

In honor of his uncle, Joseph Medicine Crow, Walks Over Ice went to Vietnam hoping to return a Crow war chief like him. Also to follow in his uncle's footsteps, he sought to perform the four types of coups needed to become a Crow war chief (see Foreword); because the Viet Cong did not have horses, however, he was unable to perform one of them. "I did take a scalp in Vietnam," he admits. "I did it because that was part of Plains Indian warfare, and I saw myself as part of that warrior tradition. I took the scalp on my very first combat action in Vietnam, in September 1966." Walks Over Ice's team of four helicopters was sent into a valley looking for a Viet Cong battalion. Because of heavy ground fire, only Carson's helicopter made it in.

The others were blown out of the air. As soon as Walks Over Ice hit the ground, he confronted an enemy soldier. "He popped up out of nowhere," Walks Over Ice says. "I shot him." The soldier was wearing a pith helmet with a red star. "As he flipped backwards, his helmet flew off and I saw he had his hair tied in a scalp lock. It was a pretty one, wrapped with beads and red flannel cloth, so I took my bayonet and cut it off."

When the non-Indian soldiers in his platoon later saw the scalp, some expressed shock. "Why did you do that? That is barbaric," they told him. "But," Walks Over Ice says, "some of them would cut ears off dead Viet Cong and say, 'This is my trophy.' Well, that scalp was my trophy. I had counted coup on that enemy, just

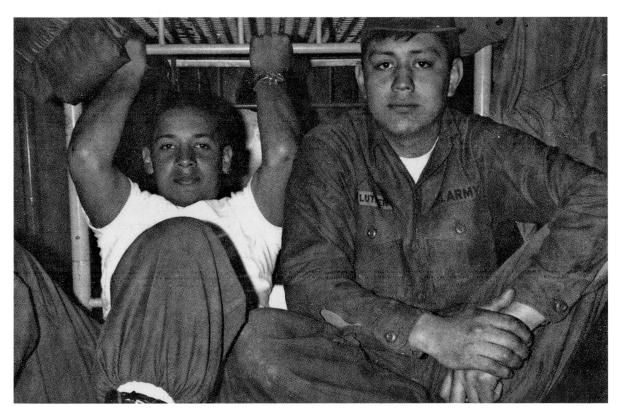

Dewayne C. Luther, Laguna-Hopi (at right), relaxes with one of his buddies in Vietnam. Luther served two tours in Vietnam in a special arms unit; he later committed suicide after his return to civilian life.

TO HONOR THOSE WHO FOUGHT

Martin Red Bear, an enrolled member of the Oglala Lakota Nation, is an artist who teaches at the Oglala Lakota College and Little Wound School in Kyle, South Dakota. A veteran of the Vietnam War, he was bothered by the fact that non-Indian veterans of that conflict generally did not receive a warm welcome or the honor they deserved when they returned home, whereas American Indians always show their respect and appreciation to their returning warriors through honoring ceremonies organized by relatives, friends, tribal veterans organizations, and warrior societies.

Red Bear's painting *"Akicita Wasté"* ("Good Soldier") is his attempt to pay tribute to these warriors. To honor today's military heroes, this unique work embodies the pictographic style made famous by the Plains Indian artists of the 19th century. It was first shown at the Northern Plains Tribal Arts Show in 1992 and now resides in the permanent collection of the Minneapolis Art Institute.

Red Bear's idea for this painting grew out of the many requests he received from various Indian and non-Indian Vietnam veterans who asked him to create simple symbols or designs in tribute to veterans for use on T-shirts, caps, women's shawls, and the like. "Composing the piece was easy," he says, "because I already knew what I wanted to do. Once I put the brush to the canvas, the images just fell into place." The circle in the top half of the painting encloses a faceless uniformed soldier holding an M16 rifle. The circle has always had spiritual significance to Indian peoples. It is a symbol of unity—the unity of family, of tribe, of country. The soldier (and other warriors in the painting), however, have no facial features. There are two reasons for this, Red Bear explains: "First, the soldier represents all who served regardless of race. Second, in some tribes, artists did not paint facial features on their human subjects for fear that doing so would remind viewers of someone they had lost and then the soul of that person could not then travel on to the next world. I believe this was and is still a part of our painting tradition."

In the background, behind the soldier, are the flags of the United States and South Vietnam as well as the symbol for the POWs and MIAs. Around the circle are unit insignias representing the five branches of the U.S. armed forces that served in Vietnam. On opposite sides of the circle are star quilt designs that symbolize the beauty in life and honor all veterans. In days past, a warrior being honored received a buffalo robe. Today the star quilt has replaced it.

A close look at the painting reveals a special emphasis on the number four, which is a sacred number to American Indians, having reference to the four cardinal points and the winds that blow from them. There are four feathers, each in a different color to represent the four colors of the human race and the four directions of the world. The four traditional dancers each have airborne unit insignias on their shields. Behind them, painted in monotone, are four animals: a buffalo representing the giver of life; a bear representing courage and bravery; a bald eagle representing the United States of America; and a golden eagle representing America's Indian peoples for whom this bird holds significant religious and spiritual meaning. All of this rests on a buffalo skull painted with

The painting *"Akicita Wasté"* ("Good Soldier") by Martin Red Bear combines Plains warrior symbols with military imagery.

various military unit insignias. On the skull are two mounted warriors with cavalry unit insignias painted on their shields.

"The title 'Akicita Wasté' ('Good Soldier') is meant to honor all the veterans of the Vietnam War regardless of their ethnicities," Red Bear affirms. "Each of them served just as courageously as the soldiers and warriors who fought in all of our country's other conflicts. In this regard, I believe 'Akicita Wasté' has fulfilled its purpose."

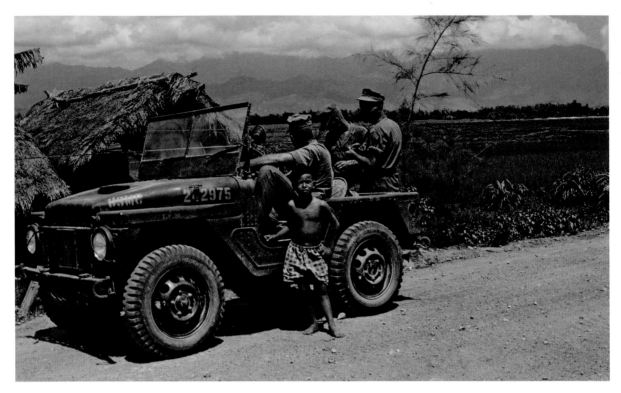

Here is "Mighty Might," the jeep that Vernon Tsoodle's squad with the 11th Marine Regiment's communications platoon used for laying wire in Vietnam. The boy in front of the jeep befriended the wiremen and often served as their interpreter.

like my ancestors did. I kept that scalp, but I blessed it with incense from sweet grass afterwards so that no bad things would come with it. I had that scalp until I got wounded and taken to Japan."

Walks Over Ice lost the scalp, but he kept its memory alive in a traditional way. After the war, a boy on the Crow Reservation needed a name. "He was a member of my clan, the Big Lodge Clan," Walks Over Ice says, "so I gave him the name 'Takes a Pretty Scalp.' Even though someone took the scalp from me after I was wounded, that name lives on among the Crow people."

Walks Over Ice brought back two other names from his tour in Vietnam. He gave the name Skydancer, after the leg-kick reaction paratroopers have when their parachute snaps open, to a nephew. He named a friend's son Kills the Pretty Enemy for the four female Viet Cong machine gunners he killed during a firefight.

During the war, M16s were used by U.S. troops. Walks Over Ice used an SKS carbine, which he had captured. The M16 "was like using a .22-caliber rifle," he says. "I shot one guy 20 times and he did not drop, so I threw that M16 away and switched to the SKS." Because the SKS was Soviet make, the only way he could get ammunition was from enemies he had killed.

Because Viet Cong snipers always tried to pick off soldiers wearing leadership insignia like stripes or bars, Walks Over Ice, like the other soldiers, never wore markings on his uniform. Instead, he tucked an eagle feather in the back of the netting that covered his helmet. With the feather sticking up, the other soldiers could recognize him in the heat of combat, especially in the jungle, where it was hard to discern the enemy. On the front was printed "Chiefie," his platoon's nickname for him. "On one side I had my wife's name, Verlie," he says, "and inside I kept her picture so I could see her every day. She was my salvation over there. She was also the one who kept me from going off the deep end when I came back. . . . Without her, I don't think I would have made it. She kept me from having bad dreams and all that kind of thing."

In the Vietnam War, it was Army policy not to put Indians together. In Walks Over Ice's company there were four Indians, one in each of the four platoons: He was in the first platoon, his friend Richard Spider was in the second, a Ponca in the third, and a Klamath in the fourth. "Even though we were often separated, it was great having Native soldiers nearby. Whenever we saw each other, we would say, 'Hey.'"

"That's a difference between Indian and non-Indian soldiers," he says. "When Indians see each other, it's like old home week. It made no difference if we were not next to each other in the field, because Indians talk with their hands, in sign language. We understand each other in sign. The non-Indian soldiers would see us doing it and say, 'What are you doing?' I'd say, 'I'm talking to him.' Even though we were 100 yards apart we could talk to each other."

As for being an Indian, Walks Over Ice felt fully accepted by his comrades. "I never noticed or experienced any discrimination, although non-Indians would look at me differently because of my name, Walks Over Ice," he says. "Most of my fellow soldiers had never met an Indian." In Walks Over Ice's experience, he and other Indians felt they had a certain reputation to live up to as Indians—that they were "a little better than everybody else, that we fought harder, that we were braver, that we were leaders."

Walks Over Ice tells of a new recruit who came up to him and said, "I am a replacement, and I want to be in your platoon." "What do you mean?" Walks Over Ice said. "You're in second platoon." "My dad was in World War II," the recruit replied, "and he said, 'If you ever get into combat, find an Indian and he will keep you alive,' so I want to be with you." "OK," Walks Over Ice said. "I'm in first; my brother Richard Spider is in second, go find him." Says Walks Over Ice, "My brother [Spider] kept him alive."

For valor under fire Walks Over Ice earned the Silver Star, the Bronze Star, and the Purple Heart. He earned the Silver Star during a search-and-destroy mission as part of a large American force seeking to intercept a North Vietnamese regiment going toward Cambodia and Laos. To reach the enemy, they had to climb a steep hill. Near the top was a long, unseen enemy trench that followed the ridgeline to the crest of the hill. As Walks Over Ice's point man tried to get his footing on the ridge, he got shot and flipped over him. "Instinctively," Walks Over Ice says, "I grabbed him by his web gear and then pulled myself up. I had my M16 in one hand and just blasted away, firing one-handed, until I ran out of ammunition, but I managed to kill all 15 guys in the trench. In the excitement of the moment I didn't even realize that I was still carrying this guy until he moaned in my ear when I finished firing. Would you believe I later saw him on a television program, so I know he survived."

As Walks Over Ice advanced up the ridge, he encountered four machine gun crews. He killed all the crews and captured the guns including a .50-caliber machine gun with an 11-man crew. When he finally reached the top, he says, 44 of the enemy were still there, including the battalion commander. They all surrendered.

WARRIORS IN UNIFORM

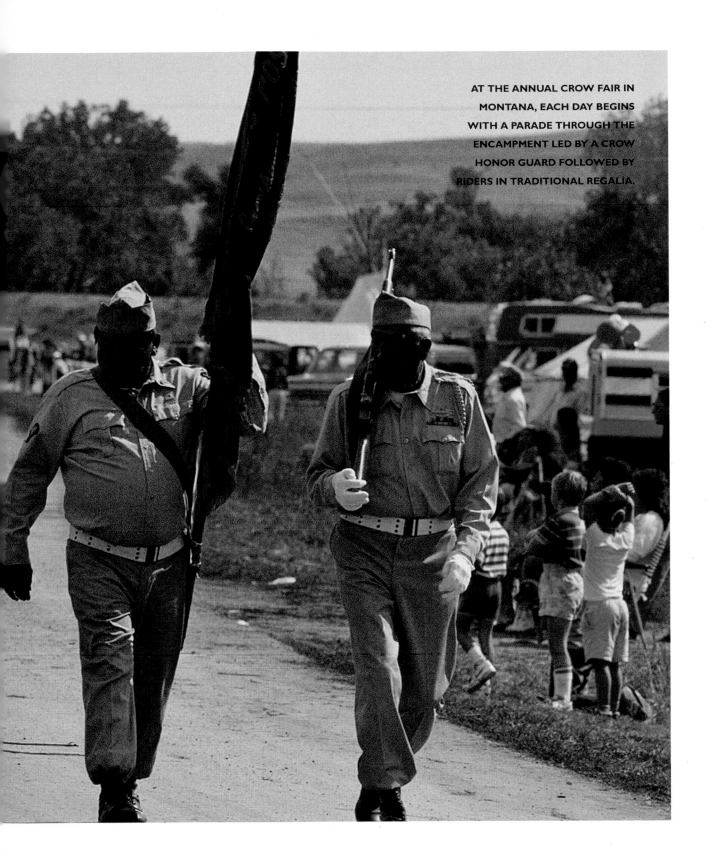

AT THE ANNUAL CROW FAIR IN MONTANA, EACH DAY BEGINS WITH A PARADE THROUGH THE ENCAMPMENT LED BY A CROW HONOR GUARD FOLLOWED BY RIDERS IN TRADITIONAL REGALIA.

Walks Over Ice was awarded the Bronze Star the following February. The objective was a suspected Viet Cong base camp. His platoon was dropped into the area following a bombing run by B-52s to sweep in and clear the area of any surviving enemy. As they moved forward after landing, an enemy machine gun opened up on Walks Over Ice. "I fell and began shooting," Walks Over Ice says. "I killed all three men in the crew and then ran over and captured the gun." As he did that, he came under fire from another machine gun to the right; suddenly the machine gun jammed. As the gunner reached over to fix it, Walks Over Ice shot him. Only then did he realize that the two machine guns were guarding a Viet Cong camp across the river and, as he says, "guys were popping out of holes all over the place." Walks Over Ice yelled to his men to follow him and began splashing across the river.

"On the other side," Walks Over Ice says, "I opened fire with the machine gun I had captured and began knocking people over. I didn't know that I was by myself until I had to stop and change ammunition belts for the machine gun. I suddenly realized that I was the only one shooting. None of my men had followed me."

Walks Over Ice got shot on his next mission. "My first stop was a hospital in the Philippines," he says. "From there I went to Okinawa, then Japan, and finally a military hospital in Denver."

The only other medal he thought he deserved but did not get was the Soldier's Medal, an award

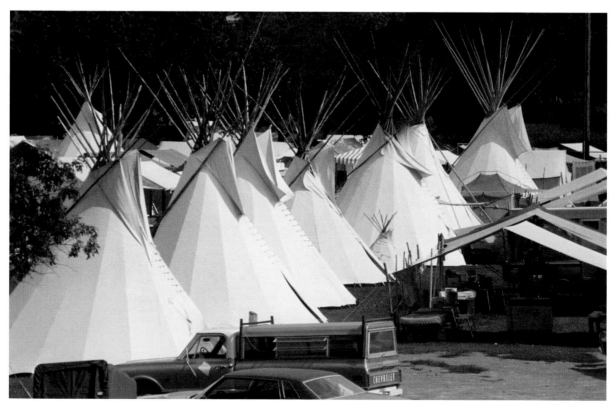

Tepees belonging to the Tsoodle family line the grounds at the Carnegie, Oklahoma, Kiowa Gourd Clan Celebration. The Tsoodles camp together there each year.

"Our People Said, 'You Did Something Good. You Did Something Great for Your People.'"

given for a noncombat heroism. In this incident some field packs caught fire and hand grenades began exploding. As the men were ran to get away, a hand grenade came flying toward Walks Over Ice and another soldier. "It was coming over our shoulders like a football," Walks Over Ice recalls. "The grenade hit the kid in the leg, knocking him down and burning his pants. I didn't want to, but I ran back and picked him up. Not until I got back to the company area did I realize I had carried him the whole way. My CO put me in for the Soldier's Medal for that particular incident, but I didn't get it. I guess," Walks Over Ice shrugs, "it was one of those things we were supposed to do because we were Indians."

Walks Over Ice's return to the reservation coincided with the annual Crow Fair. During the fair, the tribe held a ceremony for Walks Over Ice and Eddie Little Light called "the warriors' return." It is a traditional method of honoring warriors returning safely from war. Walks Over Ice says,

> At sunrise one morning the old men took us to the top of the ridge above the camp where all these teepees are. We were all on horseback. The old men then paraded us through the camp singing warrior honor songs and waking everybody up. The people then followed us into the dance arbor where we sat on our horses next to our womenfolk while the old men danced with rifles. As they danced, they sang, "This is what our men did." The dancers performed a pantomime of the deeds that each of us did in battle while an announcer described our war deeds. They told the spectators that we were defending our families, our people, and our country.

For Walks Over Ice and his fellow warriors in uniform the homecoming was different from that of the non-Indian. "Our people," Walks Over Ice recounts, "said, 'You did something good. You did something great for your people.' . . . The respect and honor we received helped a lot of the bad things we experienced to go away."

Despite the encouraging homecoming, the trauma of some experiences lingered. For Walks Over Ice the most traumatic was the death of his buddy Richard Spider. Their last battle took place when their company was ambushed while on a search- and-destroy mission. Three of the four Indians in the company were hit. Spider, who was scheduled for discharge in three weeks, was killed, as was the Klamath, and Walks Over Ice's right leg was shattered. The Ponca was the only Indian left standing.

After Walks Over Ice returned home, he visited Spider's family at Fort Thompson in South Dakota and, as part of the Indian tradition of replacing a lost loved one, was adopted by them. "Richard's dad," Walks Over Ice explains, "took me as his son because we had served together, his boy and me, and I named my middle son Richard because of him. He was a good man and a good soldier. He got the Bronze Star and a Purple Heart. For some reason, he knew he was going to die and I was going to make it. Richard's not here and I am, but his name lives on with my son."

THE POWER OF MEDICINE

Our warrior beliefs come down to us in stories. I'm descended from a line of Crow chiefs. My great-grandfather fought in the Indian wars. My grandfather was in the First World War. My dad was in World War II. My uncle was in Korea. Growing up, I was taught that joining the military was how you became a warrior, how you showed your pride in being a Crow. The warriors in our tribe dance to their honor songs. The little boys listen to their war stories. As a little boy you say to yourself, I can do the same thing. One day I will go to war and defend our people.

In the old days, Crow warriors defended their people and their land from enemy tribes, but now that the intertribal war days are over we have to go into the military in order to do our warrior deeds. Even though the Crow people have suffered much at the hands of the United States government, we accept the responsibility to fight the enemies of our country instead of enemy tribes. I could have gone to Canada like the white boys who were afraid to fight, but no, it was my turn. I knew I had to go to Vietnam because of the warrior traditions in my family and my tribe. Besides, I wanted to count coup, to do my war deeds. The only way I could do that was to go to Vietnam and be part of the action. I volunteered to go, unlike the other guys who flew with me to Vietnam. Everyone else on that plane had been drafted.

However, I felt I had an advantage over the non-Native soldiers in Vietnam because of my Indian heritage. The spirit world is very important to us and it is hard to find anyone who does not believe in the One Above, the creator. Native spiritual powers protected me and gave me peace of mind. For example, while in Vietnam I carried two powerful "medicines." I got them both from my grandmother. One was like a St. Christopher's medal with wings on it that I wore around my neck. The other one was made for me by a Crow medicine woman. I wore it on a string around my waist. I lost both of them in one fight. They were shot off by machine gun bullets. The bullets zipped around me and through my clothing, but none touched me, although one tore off my wristwatch. Another bullet came through my shirt and ripped away the medal hanging around my neck, and another one clipped off the medicine tied around my waist. Those two medicines protected me. Not a bullet hurt me. Hard as it is to believe, the medicine that had been tied around my waist came home, all the way back to Pryor, Montana, without me. The woman who made it said that it just appeared one day. These things happen. Non-Indians can't understand them, but they happen.

Another comfort to me was the ceremony in which one of my uncles prayed for my safe return. The ceremony was the Sun Dance. Because I was going overseas, my uncle danced for me, and after the ceremony, I went to him to give him cigarettes and all the other things that you give to a sun dancer. As I walked up, he said, "I saw you on crutches standing in the sunlight at the entrance to Sun Dance lodge." I knew then that I was going to be hurt in Vietnam, but that I would make it back. The next time my uncle saw me, I was on crutches because I had been shot through the leg. Those three things, the two medicines and the Sun Dance, they protected me. They brought me back.

—*Carson Walks Over Ice*

Carson Walks Over Ice mimes a Vietnam exploit at the Crow Fair. Women in war bonnets portray Viet Cong. Walks Over Ice's war shirt was made by his mother according to a dream he received in Vietnam.

Carson Walks Over Ice (far left), who frequently participates in honor guard ceremonies on the Crow Reservation, was recognized on his return from Vietnam in the ceremony held for wounded veterans.

JAMES CHASTAIN'S STORY

Carson Walks Over Ice enlisted in the 82nd Airborne to follow in the warrior tradition of his Crow people. James Chastain, a Lumbee Indian from North Carolina, enlisted in the 82d Airborne to escape the hardscrabble life on his grandfather's tobacco farm in the segregated South. This is his story.

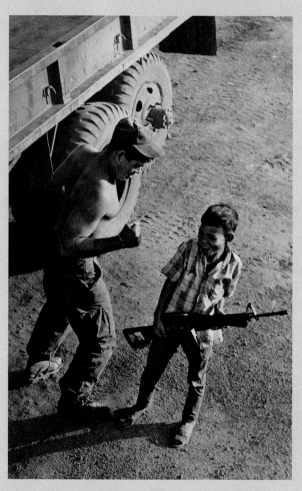

James Chastain, with the 173rd Airborne Brigade in Vietnam, plays with an orphan his group nicknamed "Jim."

I was born on my grandfather's farm on May 25, 1950, in Robeson County, North Carolina, in the heart of Lumbee country. There was no hospital and no doctor. I was delivered by an elderly Indian "Granny Woman" who was self-taught. That's the way it was done in North Carolina back then if you came into the world as an Indian. My grandfather was one of the few Indians who owned his land, and he was well thought of in our county. If you needed help, legal or illegal, you came to Mr. Will, as my grandfather was called. I can remember as a young boy Indian men coming to him for help, usually to borrow a mule or money. In return he demanded they vote his way, which was in support of the Democrat Party. My grandmother, Mary Sue Burnette, was also a full-blooded Lumbee. I was told that she gave birth to my mother in the morning and was in the fields in the afternoon.

I was mostly brought up by grandparents. My father was a soldier and served in the Korean conflict and later did two tours in Vietnam. I was one of nine children. My mother wanted me to get to know more of my siblings and other kinfolk in the Indian community around Robeson County, and at age 12 I was sent to live with my grandfather, where I began working on the tobacco farms. If you worked hard you could make three or four dollars a day, but I couldn't wait to get off the farm. I enlisted in the Army right after high school when I was 17.

As soon as I turned 18, I shipped out to Vietnam, arriving in Cam Ranh Bay on November 22, 1968. From there I was sent up to the 173rd Airborne Brigade at An Khe in the Central Highlands. I felt pretty proud to be coming to this unit because of its combat history. I was assigned to a rifle platoon running patrols in the Cha Rang Valley north of An Khe. On patrols, I was usually the point man, a position I liked and succeeded at. There was not a long list of men who wanted to walk point. Maybe it was my Indian heritage, but it was for me.

My first year in Vietnam was really tough. Somebody came up with the saying, "It ain't nothing," which we all said when things got really rough, and then we pushed on. We had a lot of contact with the Viet Cong and North Vietnamese, but most of the time we did not know who the enemy was until they started shooting at us. It only took me seven months before I was wounded and medevaced to Japan. After three months in hospital, I was deemed fit and returned to my unit. Vietnam then became a way of life for me. I stayed with the 173rd for a total of 33 months.

I received a lot of awards that first year. I got a Bronze Star, an Army Commendation Medal with a V device, a Presidential Unit Citation, the Vietnamese Cross of Gallantry, a Purple Heart, a Vietnamese Service Medal, the Combat Infantryman Badge, and the Air Medal. I also made sergeant. When I was due to rotate out my brigade commander offered me the opportunity to stay as an instructor at the Brigade Jungle School, and I took him up on it. I stayed at the school until we rotated to Fort Campbell, Kentucky, in August 1971.

My best friend in Vietnam was a young draftee, Rodney Hayden, from St. Louis, Missouri. He was the first white guy I ever called a close friend, and he is still my best friend 40 years later. When I grew up in Lumberton it was segregated. We did not associate with blacks and they did not associate with us. We did not associate with whites and they did not associate with us. Indians fought local and state ordinances that labeled Indians with blacks as "colored people."

The result of that was a tri-racial system, and we Lumbees were on the bottom of the pecking order. Indians, blacks, and whites in Robeson County had different schools, different bathrooms, different stores. The Army was the first time that I saw all races living in proximity. At first I found it strange, but due to circumstances we normally "came together" through shared hardships. On R & R, however, the different groups stuck together, but being the only Indian I was often alone. Many people asked me if I was a Mexican, especially the soldiers from Texas.

Soon after I returned to the States, I was assigned to the newly created Army Recruiting Command. The draft had ended and the Army now had to recruit its soldiers. I at first objected, but I had little choice so I became a recruiter. I spent two years in Springfield, Illinois, and then the Army sent me back to Lumberton, where, I later found out, they thought a Native Indian recruiter would boost the enlistment numbers.

The Army knew what it was doing. Recruiting became pretty easy for me. I knew most of the educators in the area and I had something to offer the young men and women in the nearby counties. By this time the three school systems—white, black, and Indian—had become one, but the Indian schools still seemed to be mostly Indian and I concentrated my efforts there. I could offer these young people so much more in the Army, and there was a trust bond. I became the Army's top recruiter the second year I was there. I worked at it around the clock. I tried to give personal care to each of my recruits. I stayed in recruiting the rest of my career and I excelled at it, becoming—at age 35—the youngest command sergeant major in the Army. I was 39 when I retired.

Being an Indian and having the warrior mentality helped me succeed, not just as a recruiter but as a soldier. Being a warrior means being out front, taking on challenges, setting the example, and never asking a soldier to do something that you would not do first.

THE PLAINS TRADITION

Among Native tribes, war deeds have long been documented by Native artists, in ledger drawings, tepee covers, winter counts, and clothing. A warrior could record his war deeds or commission an artist to do so. For the 2001 annual Northern Plains Tribal Art Show in South Dakota, I decided to create a tepee honoring Lakota Vietnam veterans, and one in particular—Charles Pablo, my uncle. My uncle Charlie had served three tours of duty in Vietnam, and at one point was missing in action. He carried the Lakota name Tagani Kopi Shi (Afraid of Nothing). After his second tour of duty, when I was in high school, he signed up to go back; I asked him why. He said he wanted to serve again so that I wouldn't have to. I didn't have to serve, and would watch U.S. involvement end as a freshman in college. My piece for the show, "Honoring Our Lakota Vietnam Veterans," consists of four dolls dressed in Army uniforms, and female dolls in traditional dress. Their waving gestures indicate that a family member has performed a brave deed such as serving in the military. I don't believe that my uncle would say that he had accomplished any great deeds while he served in the military, but I believe that he carries on a long tradition of the Plains warrior, to guard and protect the people, which I have tried to reflect in my art.

—*Emil Her Many Horses*

"Honoring Our Lakota Vietnam Veterans" places a Plains Indian tradition into a contemporary context.

"GOING TO THE OGLALA NATION PARADE"

This piece represents the changing role of the warrior and of the horse in Lakota culture. Today, both men and women serve in all branches of the military; and the horse is now represented by the automobile.

CONTEMPORARY WARRIOR

This doll depicts a Lakota soldier in the digital camouflage uniform of Iraq. He wears Lakota-style beaded moccasins, long braids, and dog tags.

CPL. NATHAN GOOD
IRON, OR YOUNG EAGLE,
A MEMBER OF THE THREE
AFFILIATED TRIBES, WAS
KILLED BY A ROCKET-
PROPELLED GRENADE IN
AFGHANISTAN IN 2006.

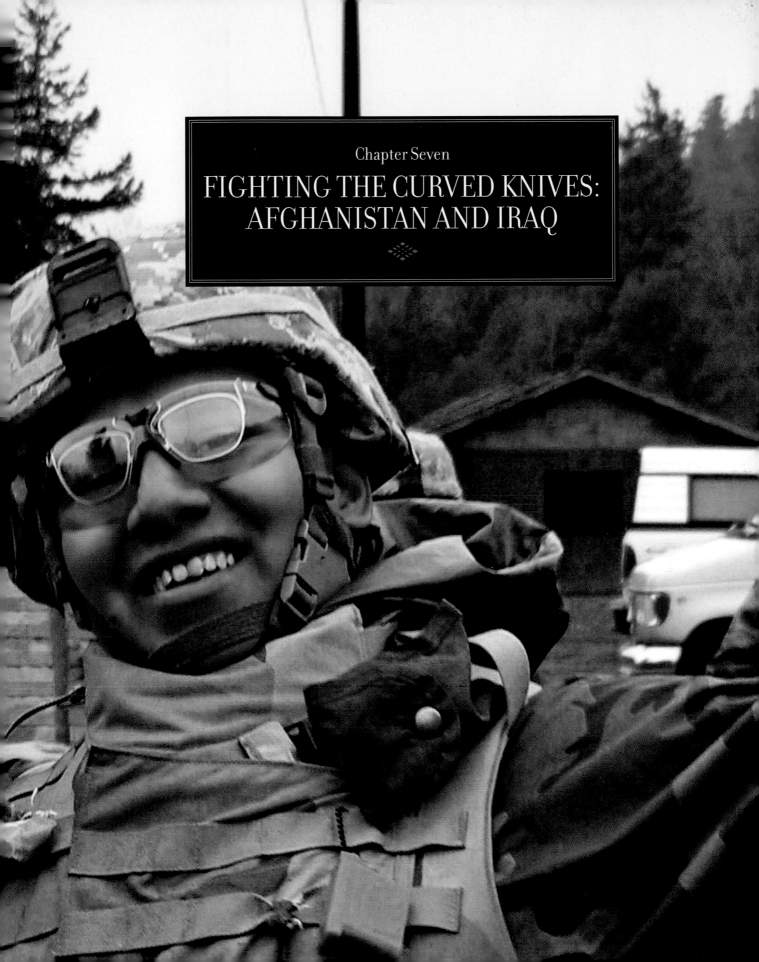

Chapter Seven

FIGHTING THE CURVED KNIVES:
AFGHANISTAN AND IRAQ

THE SETTING SUN IN
FALLUJAH, IRAQ, CASTS
A GLOW ON A HAWK
FEATHER, A SACRED
OBJECT OWNED BY
COMBAT PHOTOGRAPHER
CHUCK BOERS.

In Afghanistan and Iraq, American Indian men and women continue to serve in the armed forces in record numbers. A December 2005 tally by the Defense Department put the number of Native American/Alaskan Natives serving in the armed forces at almost 20,000. These conflicts, however, are unlike any other in America's military history. The enemy is zealous, elusive, and seldom in uniform. More often than not, the enemy arsenal consists of suicide bombers, booby traps, and hidden explosives. It is a type of warfare where "counting coup" is virtually impossible against a faceless enemy who mingles freely within a civilian population.

FOLLOWING TRADITION

Another significant difference is the ability to communicate directly with soldiers in the war zones, thanks to the Internet. A number of Native soldiers are willing—even eager—to share their thoughts about following in a warrior tradition that is ages old, even though most are far removed from their traditional culture.

One of them is Army Specialist Benji Swanson, an Ojibwe from Leech Lake, Minnesota: "Where I grew up is now over run with drugs," he writes from Iraq. "I joined the military to get away for that and not expose my kids to it. I practiced the culture for a while and then it kind of faded away. I don't dance or drum, but I do see myself as a warrior—not just for other Indians but for myself."

His sentiments are echoed by Marine Sgt. James Dunham, an Apache:

I entered the Marine Corps in December of 1995 out of pride for my namesake and uncle, James. F Bishop, who served the corps during WWII as a communications wireman. I also have a firm belief that we as citizens owe a blood debt to our nation and to our ancestors. I was a teenager before I learned that First Nation blood ran through my veins from my mother, who was part Apache. Only when I pressed family members did I start to learn the truth. As a child, I would walk into the wild by myself and find deer, porcupine, falcons and just sit and watch them for hours on end and never understand why. When the hunting season would start, my father would take me with him, although I did not hunt. He would call me his good luck because I could find game animals faster than he could. He never could figure it out why I was good at it. Honestly, I don't know either.

Although raised Christian and I have attended only one powwow—when I was five years old—I consider myself a Warrior. Yes, I do. After 9/11, I did not wait to be called up. I wanted to be on the warpath like everyone else did, so I sent a letter to the sergeant major of the Marine Corps. Five days later I received a letter from his office, and two days later, I was on orders and on an Installation Reaction Force. Now I get restless if I am home too long, knowing that there is still the fire within me to fight and my brother

"I Get Restless If I Am Home Too Long, Knowing That There Is Still the Fire Within Me to Fight."

Marines are still fighting. Because of that and my wife's support, I have deployed to Iraq in 2003, 2005, and now in 2007. Now I know what my Uncle James felt, and why he fought my grandmother so hard for permission to join the Marines when he was only 17 years old.

Sgt. Barry Crawford, a Cherokee in the Army National Guard from Oklahoma who has served three tours in Iraq, says, "I do practice some of the prayers, and some of [the] traditions." In fact, he carried a medicine bundle with him on his second tour.

It was made for me a long time ago by a Cherokee medicine woman from the Webbers Falls area of Oklahoma. It was tied at the top in the traditional way with a leather thong. When I left Kuwait to return home, a customs agent made me open it. This, of course, is very much against my beliefs. I was really upset, so I chose not to bring a medicine bundle with me on this deployment for that very reason. I already regret that decision.

More typical of today's Indian soldiers is Lucien "Luke" G. Rice III. Although he is an enrolled member of the Southern Cheyenne and Arapaho tribes of Oklahoma, his is a blended heritage of Cheyenne, Pawnee, Otoe, Pottawatomi, Sac and Fox, and German. Writing in April 2008, he says, "I am in Iraq now with several deployments under my belt. This is the longest one to date. I am a First Sergeant in a Medical Support Company with the 101st Airborne Division Warfighters."

Like so many Native soldiers, Sergeant Rice is continuing a family legacy of service in our nation's armed forces. One relative, Harvy Goodbear, was killed in Germany in World War I. An uncle, Robert Blackwolf, served with Merrill's Marauders in Burma and China in World War II. Another uncle, Dan Blackwolf, served with the 82nd Airborne in Korea. Two uncles, Eddie and Robert Wilson, are Vietnam veterans. His father, Lucien Rice, Jr., is a veteran.

And Sergeant Rice is himself a career soldier who—"all through my 21 years of service"—has followed the Native American Warrior Spirit as taught him by his father and his uncles. "They would always sit me down and tell me how important it is to keep that part of my heritage close to me during my time in the Army," says Rice.

What sustains him and his fellow American Indian soldiers, he says, is their traditional culture. "We may not always have the family life or support back at home, but we all have some traditional American Indian culture. I can always tell another Native just by watching him.

"We all have the proud Warrior tradition ingrained in us," Rice continues. "We don't have to read a creed or be taught values. We already have the willingness to engage the enemy in battle, not that we are warmongers or death dealers. It is that we have a different way of looking at war or armed conflict. Through our tribal societies and clans we already have the qualities of a Warrior—Strength, Honor, Pride, Devotion, and Wisdom—passed on to us from our elders and teachers of the Indian way. Our spiritual, physical, and mental strength follows from that."

It is not an easy life, Sergeant Rice admits. Iraq is a scary place. "You don't know if you are going to get to make it back inside the wire without being hit by an IED or enemy fire, or, if you make it back, when a round is going to fall out of the sky day or night and cause death and destruction. It is also hard on your loved ones back in the States, because all they see on television are the bad things that go on here.

"But we are here to fulfill a purpose," he concludes, "to fight and defend our homeland. And I can say this proudly: Native American Warriors do their duty with a cultural purpose that is deeply rooted in tradition and pride. This is what it means to me to be a Native American Warrior in today's Army."

As of May 2008, 48 Native Americans had been killed in Afghanistan and Iraq. One was Pvt. 1st Class Lori Piestewa, who died in Iraq in 2003. Half Hopi and half Hispanic, Piestewa has received national recognition as the first American Indian woman killed in combat. The 23-year-old soldier from Tuba City, Arizona, a mother of two, died from injuries when her unit, the 507th Maintenance Company, was ambushed near Nasiriyah.

Besides being the first Indian woman to die in combat, Piestewa now has another claim to fame:

The Shadow Wolves, traditionally trackers of drug smugglers, have taught police units in countries bordering Afghanistan how to track members of al Qaeda.

WARRIORS IN UNIFORM

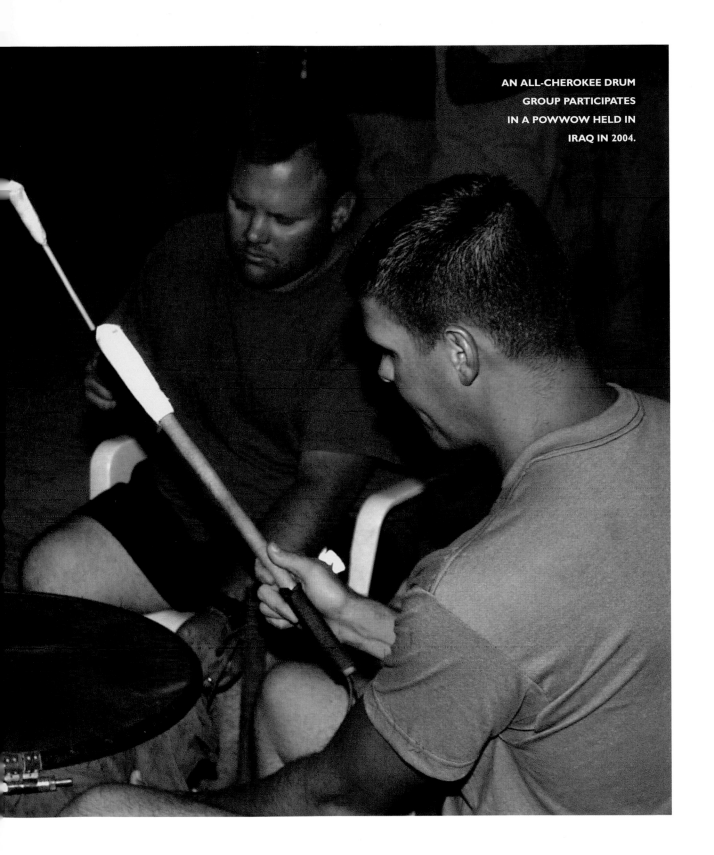

AN ALL-CHEROKEE DRUM
GROUP PARTICIPATES
IN A POWWOW HELD IN
IRAQ IN 2004.

"Squaw Peak," formerly the offensive and controversial name of the mountain summit near Phoenix, is now "Piestewa Peak" in her honor.

Another was Nathan Good Iron, a corporal in the First Battalion of the North Dakota National Guard's 188th Air Defense Artillery, who died while on patrol in Afghanistan on Thanksgiving Day 2006 when a rocket-propelled grenade struck his vehicle. Good Iron, whose Indian name was Young Eagle, was the first member of the Three Affiliated Tribes on the Fort Berthold Reservation to die in Afghanistan and Iraq. "Young Eagle," one of his eulogists declared, "your soul now flies on the wind with your brother eagles, keeping watch on those you left behind."

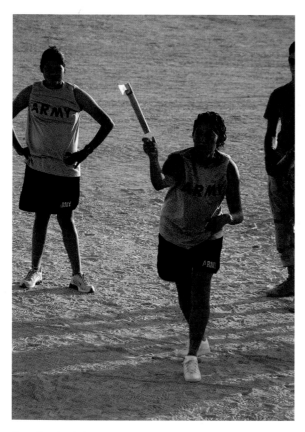

Tomahawks fashioned from scrap or truck door metal are thrown in competition at a powwow in Iraq in 2004.

THE SHADOW WOLVES

Ironically, even though much of the weaponry in use in the Middle East is on the cutting edge of technology, reflecting the computer-driven world of the 21st century, the Pentagon again has called upon American Indians to apply skills honed in another era to solve a modern military problem. Instead of needing code talkers, the U.S. Army now needs trackers who can find an enemy that eludes radar, motion detectors, cameras, and laser technology.

Alarmed at the ease with which Taliban and al Qaeda fighters were slipping in and out of Afghanistan and Iraq, the Pentagon in early 2007 sent an elite group of well-trained Native American marksmen and trackers to teach their skills to police units in Tajikistan and Uzbekistan, which border Afghanistan.

Known as the Shadow Wolves, the special unit was recruited from several tribes, including the Apache, Blackfeet, Cheyenne, Lakota, Navajo, and Tohono O'odham. Highly skilled in an ancient art and reminiscent of the Apache scouts who helped the U.S. Cavalry capture Geronimo a century earlier, the Shadow Wolves are expert at noticing clues like twigs snapped by a passing person and pieces of fabric or strands of hair snagged on a branch. The professional trackers can tell how long a sliver of food has lain in the dirt or if someone has tried to conceal his tracks by strapping pieces of carpet to his shoes.

The Shadow Wolves were actually formed in the 1970s to help Drug Enforcement Agency officials track smugglers across hundreds of square miles of the Tohono O'odham tribal reservation, southwest of Tucson, Arizona. The Shadow Wolves use the skills they often learned as children tracking game animals on the reservation or finding free-ranging livestock that may have wandered away. "Instead of tracking an animal,

"The Beat of the Drum Is a Part of the Heartbeat of a Native American."

we now track human beings," says Bryan Nez, one of the Shadow Wolves. To qualify for the special unit, recruits must be one-quarter Indian.

Although Indians today are at the heart of the modern Army, old stereotypes are hard to erase. Sgt. Eli Painted Crow, a Yaqui soldier from Arizona who served in Iraq in 2004, in an interview on Democracy Now! recalled a military briefing that warned of the dangers out in "Indian country." "They called enemy territory 'Indian country,'" she said in disbelief. "I'm standing there, just listening to this briefing, and I'm just in shock that after all this time, after so many Natives have served and are serving and are dying [in the military in Iraq], that we are still the enemy, even if we're wearing the same uniform."

A POWWOW IN IRAQ

That same year some of those Native American soldiers managed to bring a little piece of real "Indian country" to Iraq by celebrating what must have been the first traditional powwow ever held in that part of the world. The goal was to promote cultural understanding of their heritage with fellow soldiers, sailors, and Marines, while bringing a piece of home to many of the Native Americans serving in Iraq.

The powwow was organized and hosted at the Al Taqaddum Air Base near Fallujah by the 120th Engineer Combat Battalion, a National Guard unit based in Okmulgee, Oklahoma. According to Army Capt. Shareen S. Fischer, the battalion chaplain and a Shinnecock Indian from New York, nearly 20 percent of the unit's

soldiers boast some Indian blood. The two-day event featured dancing and singing, games such as stickball and tomahawk throwing, and traditional foods including genuine fry bread. The powwow ended, however, not with a traditional Native American ceremony, but a military one: the retirement of the colors.

The idea came from Sgt. Debra Mooney, a Choctaw from Idabel, Oklahoma. "We're brought up with [powwows]," she explained in an article about the event. "The beat of the drum is a part of the heartbeat of a Native American," said Mooney, who realized that the unit's year-long deployment to Iraq meant that many of the Indian soldiers would miss out on their family powwows back home. "I thought it was crazy at first," said Fischer in the article, but she took the idea to the battalion commander, who approved it even though it meant holding the powwow in a combat zone.

From start to finish, however, the planners had only a five-week window. To meet the deadline, Fischer and Mooney appointed soldiers to subcommittees to speed up the process. Dances and events had to be organized and rehearsed. Some Native dress, jewelry, and other essential regalia came from families back home. Others were fashioned from scraps of cloth, trash, and scavenged military gear. The drum came from a discarded 55-gallon oil can cut in half and canvas taken from a cot. Metal salvaged from truck doors formed the tomahawks used in a throwing contest. The stickball game featured sticks made from broom handles, with the baskets made from standard issue 5-50 parachute cord.

"I Thought to Myself I Must Be Nuts Trying to Go to a Powwow in a Combat Zone."

An all-Cherokee group named Desert Thunder sang. The master of ceremonies was Staff Sgt. David Little, a Seminole. Head dancer for the powwow was 19-year-old Specialist George D. MacDonald, a Chickasaw from Sasakwa, Oklahoma. "I was brought up in a home where the native culture, the native spirit is very, very alive," he said in the article, "so being away from it for a long time brings you down when you think about the powwows back home."

Like MacDonald, all the Indian soldiers felt proud that they had participated in this historical event. Sgt. Barry Crawford, the Cherokee from Oklahoma, was present for only an hour or so at the end: "Mission dictated that I had other things to do at the time. But I was very impressed with the efforts of my brothers and sisters to arrange it all. The 120th Engineers is my home unit, and Sergeant Mooney is a friend of mine. I know they put a lot of effort into it, and I was very touched by it."

One of the eager participants was Master Sgt. Chuck Boers, an Army combat photographer and a Lipan Apache. His presence at the powwow was purely serendipitous. Recently returned from a combat mission in Samarra and the happy recipient of a four-day pass to Qatar, he met Betty Davis, a Cherokee soldier, as he was heading to his bunk. She asked him if he was going to the powwow at Al Taqaddum Air Base. "I thought she was pulling my leg," Boers says, but then she showed him the powwow flyer and said she was going. Since the dates for the powwow fell during his four-day leave, Boers obtained permission to change locations for his R & R and immediately jumped on a convoy going to Al Taqaddum.

En route to Al Taqaddum insurgents attacked the convoy, hitting the vehicles with small-arms fire and rocket-propelled grenades. "I thought to myself I must be nuts trying to go to a powwow in a combat zone," Boers, says, "but then outta nowhere a song popped into my head. It was ["NDN Kars"] by Keith Secola. I don't know why, but after that I knew everything was going to be OK and I was going to have a great four days."

Upon arriving at Al Taqaddum, he met Sergeant Mooney, who welcomed him and introduced him around. "It was a very surrealistic site. Here we were in the middle of a combat zone and bunch of Natives had gotten together to play stickball. Can you imagine that?" Since, to his knowledge, nothing like that had ever before been done in a combat zone, and since he is a combat photographer, Boers volunteered to document the event. "[Mooney] had dedicated the powwow to all past and present veterans—so that was the theme for the powwow. It was a way to honor our fellow warriors. We all knew this was going to be a very special event and it would be like no other powwow that any of us had ever attended."

Indeed it was—just like "Indian Fair Days [an annual powwow] back home," Boers marvels. "We played stickball and Indian marbles, and we had a tomahawk throwing and blow gun contest the first day. That night we all got together for a little bit of singing, drumming and dancing. It wasn't a 49er [a dance party held following a

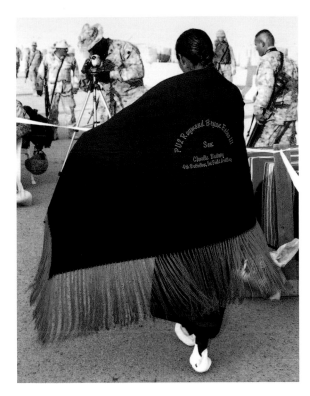

A ceremonial shawl was sent by the family of fallen warrior Raymond Bryan Estes to honor him at the 2004 powwow.

powwow] or anything like that, but it was fun just hanging together."

During the powwow the next day there was an honoring ceremony for a fallen warrior, Specialist Raymond Bryan Estes III, a Ponca, of Charlie Battery, Fourth Battalion, First Field Artillery. His family had sent over a shawl to be used during the powwow. Debra Mooney placed the shawl over Specialist Leslie Montemayor, a soldier of Creek and Seminole heritage. After receiving the shawl, Montemayor danced alone in the arena as everyone stood in honor and remembrance of their fallen brother warrior.

"The powwow was a great success," Boers says. "I was amazed at how many other Natives made the trip from all over Iraq. Most everyone had heard about the powwow by word of mouth, from a flyer, or in an email. It was just like back home."

SHARED HERITAGE

During his 20 years as a combat photographer Boers has been deployed to all of the U.S. Army's hot spots—Grenada, Haiti, Bosnia, Kosovo, and the Middle East, including three tours in Iraq, during which he has received a Bronze Star, two Army Commendation Medals, two Purple Hearts, and a Polish service medal for his work as an adviser. "Everywhere I went," Boers says, "I had always run into other Natives, and we would usually all hang out together and tell stories about powwows, 49ers, and other stuff like that, but nothing could have prepared me for my fourth tour to the Middle East during Operation Iraqi Freedom. Every Forward Operating Base or mission I went on, I would run into another Native; it was something I had never experienced in my whole military career."

One of those warriors in uniform Boers met in Iraq was Sam Stitt, a Choctaw from Oklahoma serving in the Air Force. Stitt is a military linguist fluent in Arabic, with training in Iraqi dialects. At the time he was assigned to a small team operating in south central Iraq, on a base outside of An Najaf and was there for the siege of An Najaf, in April 2004 as well as various other actions and firefights. Although some of his duties would be considered classified, he was "outside the wire" every day. "It was quite intense and actually not very fun at all," Sam admits. "I was scared to death half the time, really. I met Chuck when he came down to An Najaf for an anticipated 'action.' . . . We met up with his team and helped them get settled in. Since I was the intelligence operator, I briefed him on the general security situation in our region."

Only after working together for several days did Boers and Stitt discover their shared Native heritage. It happened because Boers wanted to check his email and Stitt had

SPC. BENJI SWANSON OF THE 1-565TH QUARTERMASTER COMPANY ATOP HIS HUMVEE EN ROUTE TO CAMP ECHO IN IRAQ.

"The Young Kids at the Gatherings or Powwows Look Up to the Vets."

Internet connection in his office. Boers, in fact, was checking out "Pow Wow Highway," a Native American website. Then Stitt noticed his Native features. "I was so excited," Stitt says. "I shouted, 'Hey, I'm an enrolled Choctaw from Oklahoma,' and I grabbed a photo of my kids in powwow regalia that I had on my desk."

They formed an immediate friendship. "In a short amount of time it felt like we had been friends for years. We would chat for hours about dancing, singing, family, and tribal issues. We talked about hitting the Pow Wow Highway together when we got home."

On the day of the mission, Boers and Stitt decided to create a wall mural (opposite), showing their tribal affiliations and marking the date and place, as a memento. They used bits of old plaster or rock from rubble to draw it, and a combat cameraman took their picture posing in front of it.

"That photo somehow got back stateside," says Stitt, "and made its way onto the cover of *Indian Country Today,* May 9, 2004. We were featured on the same page as the Navajo code talkers. What an honor! The photo also made it into my tribal paper, the *Bishinik.*"

Like his newfound friend, Stitt entered military service because, as a Native, it seemed the thing to do, although he is quick to admit that the idea of the Plains Indian in full buckskin regalia with feathers flying—the warrior image that is seared into the mainstream American consciousness—does not quite fit the Choctaw experience. "Most Choctaws are Christian or hold some hybrid Native-Christian belief," Stitt says:

We don't have the religious ceremonies for warriors one might find among the other so-called "warlike" tribes. However, the Choctaws have a long history of military service and tribal members in WWI were, in fact, the first code talkers.

It happened, Stitt was told, because a group of Okie Choctaws were chatting one day and an enterprising officer overheard them and came up with the scheme to have them send radio messages "in the clear" between Choctaw soldiers stationed at various positions on the battlefield.

Most Choctaw families, Stitt declares, have some tie to a veteran. "It's a tradition of sorts, and when I was young I just assumed that one day I would join. The young kids at the gatherings or powwows look up to the vets and it is something honorable—even if the war itself isn't. That is one reason non-Native vets show up at Native events. They know that they will get the respect they deserve, especially the Vietnam vets. Many of them had it rough fitting back into a society that could be hostile to them at times."

Like generations of warriors before him, Boers carries a medicine bundle and prepares himself spiritually before possible combat situations. These spiritual protectors he shares with Natives and non-Natives alike. For example, a month after their assignment in An Najaf, Stitt visited Camp Victory, Boers's home base near Baghdad. "We had about thirty minutes or so before Sam had to roll back out to An Najaf," Boers says, "but that was more than enough time for us to catch up on what we had both been doing."

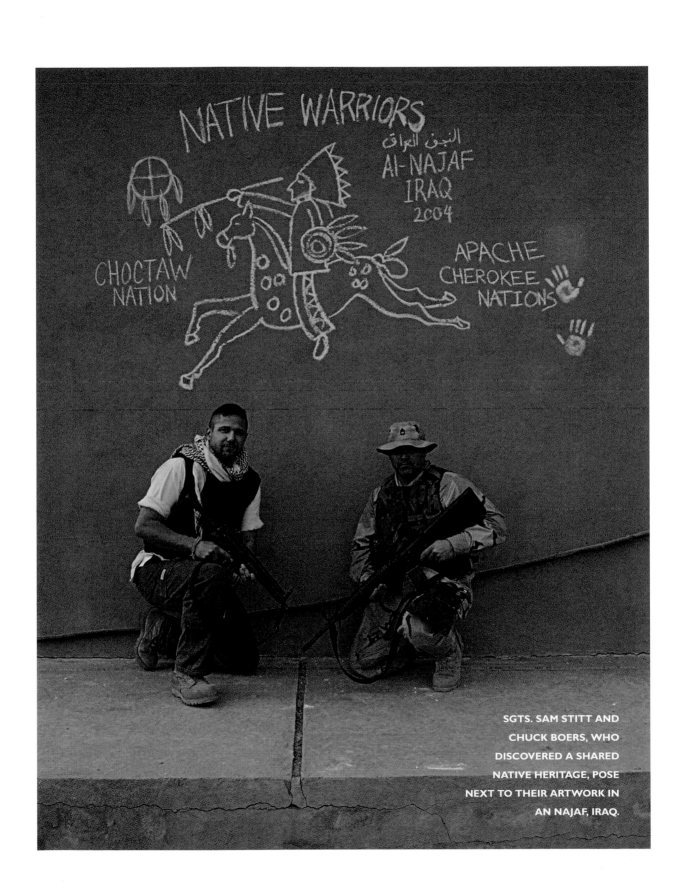

SGTS. SAM STITT AND
CHUCK BOERS, WHO
DISCOVERED A SHARED
NATIVE HERITAGE, POSE
NEXT TO THEIR ARTWORK IN
AN NAJAF, IRAQ.

TRIBAL FLAGS

The first documented use of flags by North American Indians was during the Civil War. According to Donald T. Healy, co-author of *Native American Flags,* the soldiers from the Five Civilized Tribes who fought for the Confederacy flew their own battle banner. The flag of the Choctaw Nation still features some elements of that Civil War alliance.

The Arapaho of the Wind River Reservation in Wyoming designed one of the first of the modern-era tribal flags that are in widespread use today. The flag, which was adopted in 1956, grew out of the need for an appropriate way to honor tribal veterans.

Besides promoting tribal identity, the flags are also a statement of tribal sovereignty. As Healy points out, a series of landmark federal decisions in the last quarter of the 20th century that buttressed the right of Native self-government inspired many of the tribes to design and fly their own flags. The proliferation of tribal casinos was also a factor.

Master Sgt. Chuck Boers (left) and Staff Sgt. James Dunham hold up the Lipan Apache tribal flag at Multi-National Division Central-South, Camp Echo, Ad Diwaniyah, Iraq.

"After I Finished Blessing My War Pony, the Soldiers Asked If I Would Bless Them."

Before Stitt left, Boers gave him some sage and cedar and two hawk feathers for his children. That evening, at the nightly update briefing, it was announced that a convoy going from Baghdad to An Najaf had been attacked. Boers later recalled,

My first thoughts were about Sam. That night I prayed to the Creator to look out for him. The next day when I went to check email, there was one from Sam telling me about the firefight and the attack on his convoy. It was a close one for him and the others that day. I know when Sam passes those Hawk feathers to his children it will have a very special meaning for them.

A month later, Boers was back in the fight. This time he was sent to Fallujah to photograph operations with Apache Troop, Second Battalion, Seventh Regiment, First Cavalry Division. As the three soldiers assigned to help him watched, Boers hung a hawk feather, did a small blessing with some cedar and sage, and painted the side of his "War Pony"—an armored all-terrain vehicle, which has replaced the jeep in the modern Army. He says,

I thought my soldiers would think me crazy or something as I did my Native spiritual preparations, but I didn't care. Then, to my surprise, after I finished blessing my War Pony, the soldiers asked if I would bless them. I am glad I did because it was kinda rough for us in Fallujah. The squad we were with got hit real hard and one soldier, SPC Jose A. Velez, was killed. . . . For his actions that day Velez was awarded the Silver Star along with two other members of his squad. Now when I gourd dance, I remember not only our past, present, and future warriors, but I also always remember and honor SPC Velez and the other soldiers I served with that day in Fallujah.

True to their promise in Iraq, Boers and Stitt did link up stateside and attend a few powwows together. "It was great—almost like the 'band of brothers' cliché," Stitt says. He adds,

But it's not a cliché. We exchanged gifts. He presented me with hawk feathers and an eagle spike, and I gave him a beaded knife sheath. Once he let me borrow a uniform and his Native color guard allowed me to participate in the posting of colors. Since that time I've been dancing at powwows in the Northwest and often I am asked to be a flag bearer. Several times I've been given an honor song and danced solo, with the crowd standing. It is such a great feeling.

And like Boers, Stitt also remembers fallen warriors as he dances, like fellow Choctaw Lance Cpl. Hatak Yearby, who died in a vehicle explosion in Al Anbar province in May 2006. As Stitt says modestly, "It's how Indians honor their warriors."

WARRIORS IN UNIFORM

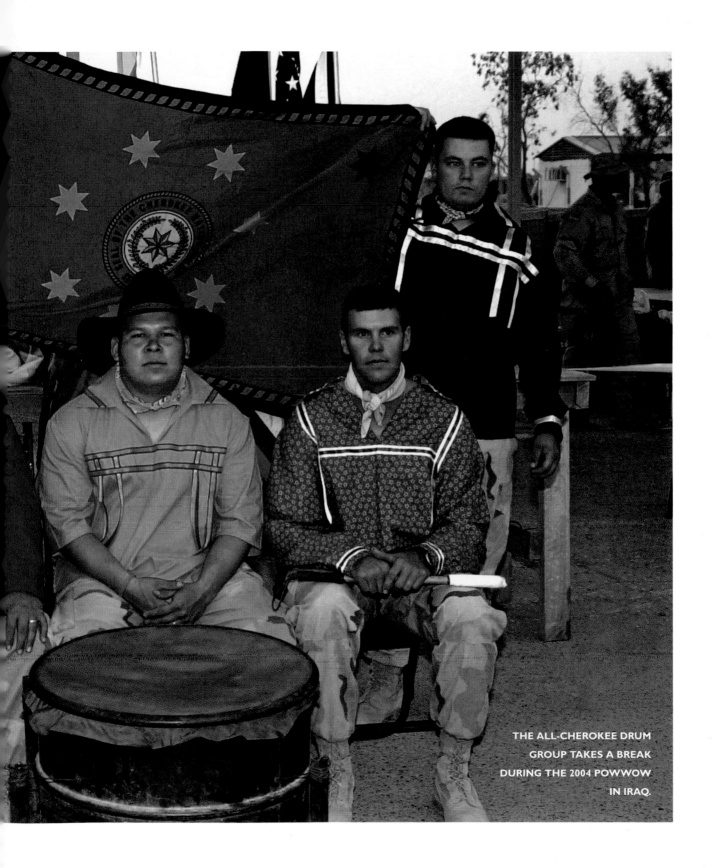

THE ALL-CHEROKEE DRUM
GROUP TAKES A BREAK
DURING THE 2004 POWWOW
IN IRAQ.

CHUCK BOERS'S STORY

Master Sgt. Chuck Boers is typical of many of today's Indian soldiers. His mother is Chiricahua/Lipan Apache and Western Band Cherokee from Oklahoma. His father is a Dutchman who came to America from Holland after World War II with his family. His parents divorced soon after he was born. While growing up, Boers learned about his Apache culture from his grandfather and his Cherokee culture from his grandmother. Although his mother's family was from Oklahoma and Texas, he grew up primarily in California. "One might think, being so far away from our tribal roots, that we would lose touch with who we are, but that was not the case. My grandparents showed and shared with me and my sisters the richness and vibrancy of our culture."

Nonetheless, it was not always easy growing up as an urban Indian, never really quite fitting in the red or white worlds. It was Boers's family and other Indian friends who helped him accept life in both worlds. He credits Betty Coulter, a Cherokee, and other Title IV (Indian Education Act) Native counselors with helping him get through his teenage years.

What stand out were the powwows, the tribal ceremonies, and Title IV events that he attended. "My favorite part of the powwow was grand entry, when the veterans would bring in the colors and then afterwards they would do an honor dance," Boers says. "I was taught that we always welcome home our warriors with songs and dances, and my thoughts always turned towards my parents, uncles, and other relatives who had served in the military. I was proud of them and of the sacrifices that they had made for all of us."

The day Boers graduated from high school and got his diploma, he was on top of the world, he says. What made the day more special and memorable, however, was that his Title IV counselor Betty Coulter gave him his first eagle feather, telling him she was proud of the young man he had become and that the feather would keep him safe while he was in the Army. "I have carried that eagle feather with me all over the world—on deployments, on peacekeeping missions, into combat, and one day after I retire," he says, "I will pass that eagle feather on to the next young warrior."

Boers joined the Army in August 1982, just before the start of his senior year of high school. His recruiter was his mother, Virginia, a sergeant first class who spent 11 of her 20 years in the Army as a recruiter. "The joke in the family was that my mother was low on her recruiting numbers that month and needed to put me in the Army in order to make her numbers," Boers says, adding,

In truth, I have always looked up to my parents and my other relatives who had served in the military. In fact, our family has served in every war that the United States has had since World War I. We even had family serve as Army scouts in the late 1800s. I wouldn't call us patriotic, but we are proud to serve our people and protect our way of life. I knew I wanted to be part of that world. It is part of our culture to be warriors.

Boers's mother did not see herself as a warrior, but she did see the Army as a unique opportunity for a woman. "It opened a lot of doors for me," she says. "Back then there weren't a whole lot of jobs for a woman that paid as well as the military and taught you a skill at the same time. While in the WACs (Women's Army Corps), I was in transportation and administration, but my last 11 years I was an Army recruiter. I was proud and pleased that Chuck was continuing our family and tribal tradition—to serve in the military."

Virginia, the oldest of five children, had four brothers, and all of them followed her into the Army. Three were combat medics and one served in the Air Defense Artillery. One served two tours in Vietnam as a Special Forces medic, followed by a tour in Desert Storm. As if a 20-year military career was not challenge enough, she also had six children of her own and raised another one as well.

Boers thanks his mother not only for getting him into the Army, but also for helping him make it through boot camp. As luck would have it, he was assigned to the same camp and same unit his mother had been assigned to when she went through basic training: Fort McCullen, Alabama, Third Platoon, Delta Company, Second Battalion. "When the training got tough, I would tell myself—'If my mom, who is less than five feet tall, did this, so can I.' It was like she was there pushing me all through basic training. I used to wonder about the odds of going through basic training in the same unit as my mother and living in the same barracks she had lived in so many years ago. My mother…felt that it would give us a different kind of bond, not only as mother and son, but also as soldiers. My grandmother had always told me the Creator had a plan and reason for everything that happens. We may not understand it at the time, but eventually it might be revealed to us. That's the only way I could explain it."

Chuck Boers received the ultimate honor in 2007 at the Annual Inter-tribal New Year's Eve Pow Wow in Fresno, California. He was home

Sgt. Chuck Boers has more than 20 years of service in the military and says, "It is part of our culture to be warriors."

on leave from his third tour to Iraq at the time. During a break in the ceremony, Lipan Tribal Chairman Daniel Romero called Boers to the center of the room for a blessing and cleansing ceremony. In the place of honor next to him stood his mother and his daughter, Christina. While Chairman Romero conducted the ceremony, Ron Goode, one of his Title IV counselors, told the audience about Boers's military exploits and his service to the Lipan people.

Boers had been told of the ceremony ahead of time, but he was not prepared for what followed. Chairman Romero bestowed upon Boers the title of Lipan War Chief and the name Nantá éé, meaning Lipan Apache Warrior Number 2. (The tribal chairman is Number 1.)

"I could not believe it," Boers says. "Our tribe has not had a war chief in over 70 years. It is a great honor to receive the title Lipan War Chief, and I could not have ever expected something like this in a million years. It is also very humbling, because there have been many great warriors in our tribe, and they have not had this honor bestowed upon them."

CARRIED ITEMS

One of the traditional strengths of Native American culture was dancing, and it remains so to this day. Indeed, one of the most visible expressions to this day is the powwow, which is at once a social gathering, celebration, family reunion, and an occasion for spiritual reunion.

Although the federal government banned such public expressions of culture at the end of the 19th century, most tribes kept the tradition alive in secret. Once the ban was lifted in 1933, dancing resumed its rightful place in American Indian life. A great impetus was the welcome home celebrations for returning World War II Indian veterans.

Dancing was a way for warriors to reenact their skill and success on the battlefield, to bring honor and glory to themselves and their families, and today's veterans carry on that timeless tradition at powwows across the country. When they dance, they often carry trophies of war or other objects that leave no doubt as to their branch of service or their military exploits.

DANCE REGALIA *(left)*

A Marine medallion on a beaded necklace, beaded pin, blanket, and gourd made from a Vietnamese hand grenade reflect veteran Vernon Tsoodle's continued devotion to the Corps.

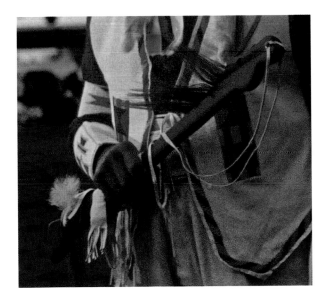

HORSE DANCE STICK *(above)*

Plains Indians made such sticks to honor a favorite war pony or memorialize an enemy horse's capture.

BUCKSKIN POUCH *(right)*

Possibly used as a medicine bundle in Vietnam, the pouch is adorned with military insignia.

AT THE OPENING CEREMONY AT
A POWWOW ON THE ROSEBUD
SIOUX RESERVATION, IN SOUTH
DAKOTA, THE VETERANS HOLD
COUP STICKS AND BOTH
TRIBAL AND AMERICAN FLAGS.

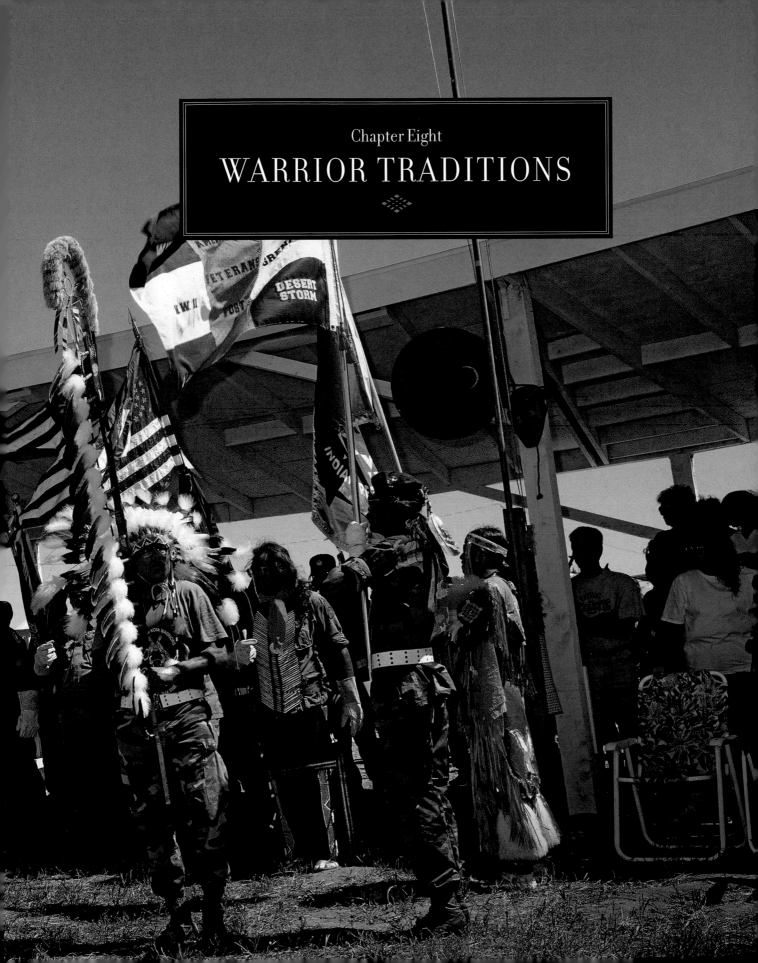

Chapter Eight
WARRIOR TRADITIONS

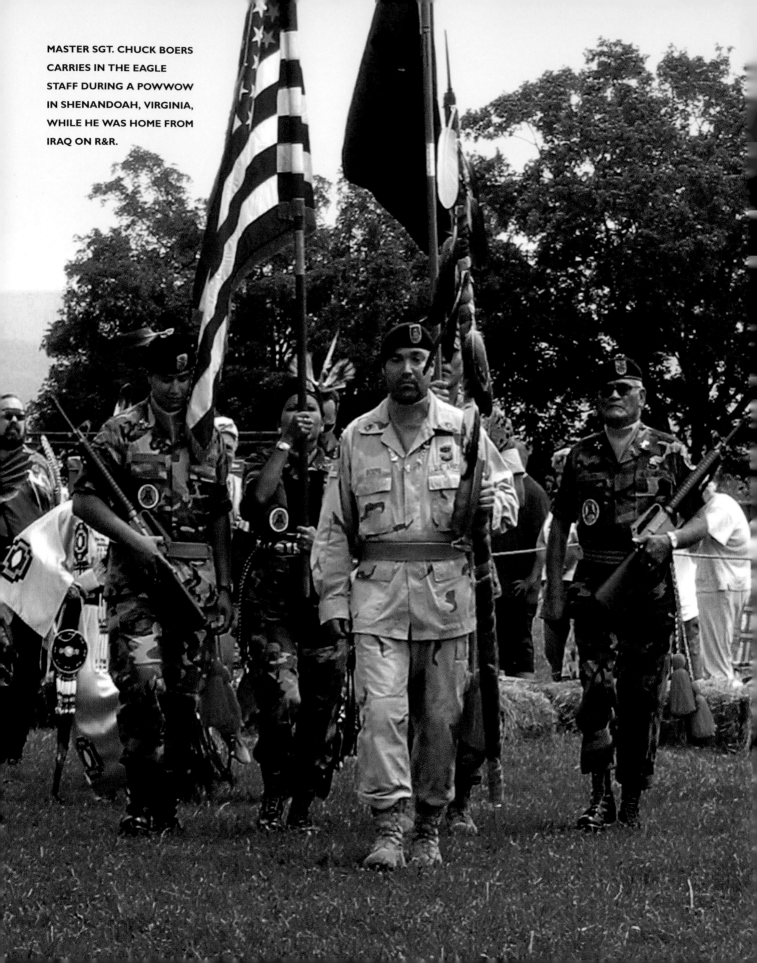

MASTER SGT. CHUCK BOERS CARRIES IN THE EAGLE STAFF DURING A POWWOW IN SHENANDOAH, VIRGINIA, WHILE HE WAS HOME FROM IRAQ ON R&R.

Native American veterans are honored by their family and their tribe, both before going into service and upon their return. The most visible expression of the honor Indian veterans receive is seen at powwows.

For Native Americans, powwows can be everything from a family reunion to a religious ceremony. Largely associated with Plains tribes, powwows were primarily spiritual gatherings to celebrate certain tribal events or individuals through songs and dancing.

When Indians were moved onto reservations at the end of the 19th century, the meaning of their dancing changed. They began to use dance—the Ghost Dance is a prime example—as a way to ask for spiritual help and guidance to cope with changes being forced on them by the U.S. government. The government, in turn, regarded the dancing as inflammatory, a hopeless attempt to hold on to a lost way of life, and banned them. The ban was eventually lifted in 1933, and dancing resumed its important position in tribal culture. Indeed, powwows today are a vital part of keeping tribal traditions alive.

At many powwows, Indian veterans are honored. They can be asked to lead the Grand Entry, to carry the tribal and U.S. flags, and to dance. In recent years, powwows dedicated to Indian veterans have appeared across the country. One of these, held annually in November, is the National Native American Veterans Pow Wow. Marine Corps Gunnery Sgt. Shawn Arnold, one of the event co-founders, told the American Forces Press Service, "We hold the powwow to pay tribute to Native Americans who put their lives at risk to ensure the survival of future generations."

One of the veterans frequently honored at powwows was Lt. Billy Walkabout, a Cherokee who is often cited as the most decorated Native American soldier of the Vietnam War. A member of Company F, 58th Infantry Regiment, 101st Airborne Division, Walkabout received the Distinguished Service Cross, the nation's second highest military award; five Bronze Stars; five Silver Stars; and six Purple Hearts, as well as the Legion of Valor and five Army Commendation Medals. A few of his heroic actions—in which he saved several of his fellow soldiers—are recounted in *Eyes of the Eagle,* by Gary A. Linderer, one of the wounded men he saved. Linderer called Walkabout "a hero earning a Medal of Honor before my eyes."

Walkabout, who died in 2007 at the age of 57, had a troubled life after Vietnam. He had medical problems related to his exposure to the defoliant Agent Orange, and he endured painful memories. "War is not hell," he told an interviewer in 1986. "It's worse." He struggled with depression and thoughts of suicide, spending months in self-isolation. He only found solace, according to his family, at powwows.

PRIVATE RITUALS

Less visible but nonetheless important to Indian military personnel are private rituals and religious ceremonies, such as the blessing Vietnam veteran Duane Simpson received before he left

The Elders Vowed, "Your Spirit and Ours Will Protect You."

his home on the Colville Indian Reservation to join the Army in 1964. Simpson's experiences were featured in one of a series of articles the Spokane, Washington, *Spokesman Review* ran on Thomas Watt, a Colville Indian who served in Vietnam.

Tribal elders took the 17-year-old boy into the mountains to purify him and prepare him spiritually. According to *Spokesman Review* writer Kevin Graman, Simpson's uncle had to break ice in a stream for the sweathouse ceremony, which included being cleansed with cedar smoke and plunging four times into the frigid water.

At the conclusion of the ceremony, the elders vowed, "Your spirit and ours will protect you." At a 2005 veterans reunion, wrote Graman, Simpson theorized that the protection he received was "as good a reason as any" for his surviving two tours of duty.

BLACK LEGGINGS SOCIETY

For the tribes with a warrior tradition, their military societies help keep that tradition alive. One of the most celebrated is the Ton-Kon-Ga, or Black Leggings Society, of the Kiowa Indian Nation of Oklahoma (see pages 202-203).

How the society got its name is unknown. Some think it derives from the trail dust that blackened the legs of warriors after a long trek. Others suggest it is in honor of Kiowa warriors who survived an attempt by enemies to defeat them by setting fire to the prairie grasses during a battle.

The society flourished during the 19th century until driven underground around 1890 by the Bureau of Indian Affairs, which sought to eradicate all forms of traditional religion practiced by America's Native peoples. By 1928, the society had ceased to function until its revitalization by Kiowa military veterans 30 years later. One of the veterans was Gus Palmer, who dedicated the revival to the memory of his brother Lyndreth, killed in World War II. Thanks to the efforts of the few surviving society members, who taught the songs, dances, and traditions to younger military veterans, the Black Leggings Society is active and vibrant.

Membership traditionally has been restricted to enrolled Kiowa (or certified tribal members), although reportedly some Comanche have become members. Members wear black leggings (or paint their legs black) and a red cape, which symbolizes the red cape captured from a Mexican army officer. The society emblem is a staff wrapped in otter fur. The society tepee features the battle designs of a famous 19th-century war chief on one side and the service crests of today's Kiowa servicemen on the other. It also features the names of the nine Kiowa servicemen killed in combat since World War I.

The society holds mourning feasts, conducts cedaring ceremonies, and performs graveside tributes for deceased members. At each biannual ceremony the society provides a meal to all in attendance. Female relatives of society members perform scalp and victory dances using men's lances and feathered headdresses to open the afternoon events, while inside the tepee the men prepare for the five types of dances they will

Women perform at a Kiowa Black Leggings ceremony. The society, which had all but disappeared 100 years ago, has been revitalized by Kiowa military veterans in the past 50 years.

perform. Once a year the society performs the Tsat'hoigya, or Reverse Dance, during which a combat veteran stops the drum and recites a personal battle exploit.

The society's most distinguished member was First Sgt. Pascal Poolaw. A veteran of three wars—World War II, Korea, and Vietnam—Sergeant Poolaw is acclaimed as America's most decorated "warrior in uniform." He earned 42 medals, badges, citations, and campaign ribbons for combat service and for valor, including three Silver Stars, five Bronze Stars, three Purple Hearts (one in each war), three Army Commendation Medals, and the Distinguished Service Cross. He was also nominated for the Medal of Honor.

Although Sergeant Poolaw had retired in 1962, he reentered the Army five years later in an effort to keep his son Lindy from having to go to Vietnam. Another son, Pascal Poolaw, Jr., had already served in Vietnam, losing a leg in an explosion, and Army regulations prohibited two members of the same family from serving in a combat zone without their consent. But Sergeant Poolaw was too late. Upon reaching the point of departure on the West Coast, he discovered that Lindy had left for Vietnam the day before, so he decided to follow him.

Having father and son in combat at the same time was nothing new to the Poolaw family. Pascal had served in World War II with his father

GRAYHORSE AMERICAN WAR MOTHERS' SOLDIER DANCE

The Grayhorse American War Mothers are members of the American War Mothers (AWM), a federally chartered patriotic organization founded during World War I. At one time Oklahoma boasted 23 chapters. Now only a few exist in Indian communities—Kiowa, Otoe, Pawnee, two Osage, Mi-tho-to-moie, and Grayhorse chapters. Their continued existence is evidence of the high regard Indian people still retain and proudly exhibit for their military veterans.

One way in which the Grayhorse War Mothers continue to honor their veterans is to host a Soldier Dance each year on Mother's Day weekend. The dance is not a powwow, although a master of ceremonies and an arena director are present to direct and clear the way for the organized and traditional ceremonies that follow the flag raising.

After the opening prayer song, the veterans parade in with the War Mothers and circle the drum, stepping to its beat and rhythm. Families sing songs honoring individual Osage veterans. These songs were given to Grayhorse War Mothers from the repertoire of war dance songs handed down from generation to generation. New mothers are carefully reminded that Grayhorse chapter members treasure these songs because they have been entrusted with them. There is an obligation to keep them alive to honor the memories of those who gave so much for the Osage Nation and the country.

Taking care of the songs consists of not only honoring veterans with the annual singing of their songs at the Soldier Dance, but also—in a very traditional way of Indian people—providing a feast for veterans, families, and friends. Because Osage veteran ceremonies are so family focused, the families of veterans with songs naturally share in the care of the songs. Osages are happy to give to families and friends of veterans who have served and sacrificed for their country. Typical of Indian generosity, many gifts entail financial sacrifice, such as a quarter side of beef or Pendleton blankets.

One special tradition during the Soldier Dance is to give a dollar or more to a family after dancing to the veteran's honor song. This act allows anyone to express honor and to help families take care of their veteran's songs. These gifts make it easier for the veteran's family to thank the drum group appropriately for playing the song, to recognize special people in their lives, or to honor a new or a deserving veteran. They say this completes the circle. Some call this a "giveaway," but essentially it is a means of ensuring that our honor songs are preserved and cared for.

The singers and dancers, the givers, and the tellers of war and honor stories are active all afternoon. When they are finished, the colors are retired and a prayer ends the ceremonies before supper. There is a tradition at Osage veteran feasts, although it is probably not traditional as meant in "old Indian ways" and may not even be strictly Osage: Grayhorse War Mothers bring cakes decorated with their veteran's name and rank, company or platoon, branch of service and dates served, and sometimes even edible photos. The patriotic cakes are proudly lined up on long tables for all to see. Guests enjoy gathering around the red, white, and blue decorated cakes and talking about the veterans they memorialize, while the mothers and other family members of the veteran enjoy having their loved one remembered and their cakes admired.

Grayhorse War Mothers wear ceremonial shawls as they participate in an annual Soldier Dance, held every Mother's Day weekend. Traditional songs, dances, prayers, and stories honor war veterans.

The day's festivities conclude with a War Dance. Some might think this part of the day's activities is a powwow because some of the participants, especially the young ones, are dressed in traditional Osage clothes and engage in considerable socializing as well as dancing. This is where the similarity ends, because the War Dance—unlike a powwow—ends at a reasonable hour. But whatever one chooses to call this part of the festivities, one thing is certain: Cultural traditions and practices are being maintained, protected, and carried on for future Osages. Men and boys will put on their moccasins and broadcloth leggings tied down with large bells. They will slip into long and blousy shirts fastened with metal armbands and wide beaded belts to contain the fullness, attach roaches and feathers, and carry in their hands weapons, war whistles, or, of all things, a mirror. (Osages are said to have once been arrogant and vain, and some people say they remain so to this day.) Ladies and young girls, too, dress in their traditional Osage clothes.

The Soldier Dance is just one ceremony at which the tribe honors its veterans. Another is the "Inlonska" (playground of the oldest son), which is a ceremonial dance of the entire Osage Nation, held each June. Although the Grayhorse War Mothers do not sponsor the dance, we support and participate in it. During a recent Osage Inlonska, a young tribal member, David Travis Meneely, who had been deployed in Iraq, performed. While he danced, he carried a red-and-white-checked head wrap that he had probably taken during combat. Obviously, it held much meaning for this veteran.

The Grayhorse War Mothers are proud to have a role in honoring our veterans and continuing the cultural traditions that live on from the ancient War Dance days of our Osage warriors. The passage of time, of course, has brought with it changes due to the emergence of new memorable experiences and has given them special meaning. The use of the American flag, I am sure, is one of those changes.

—*Toy Kelly, Past President*

WARRIORS IN UNIFORM

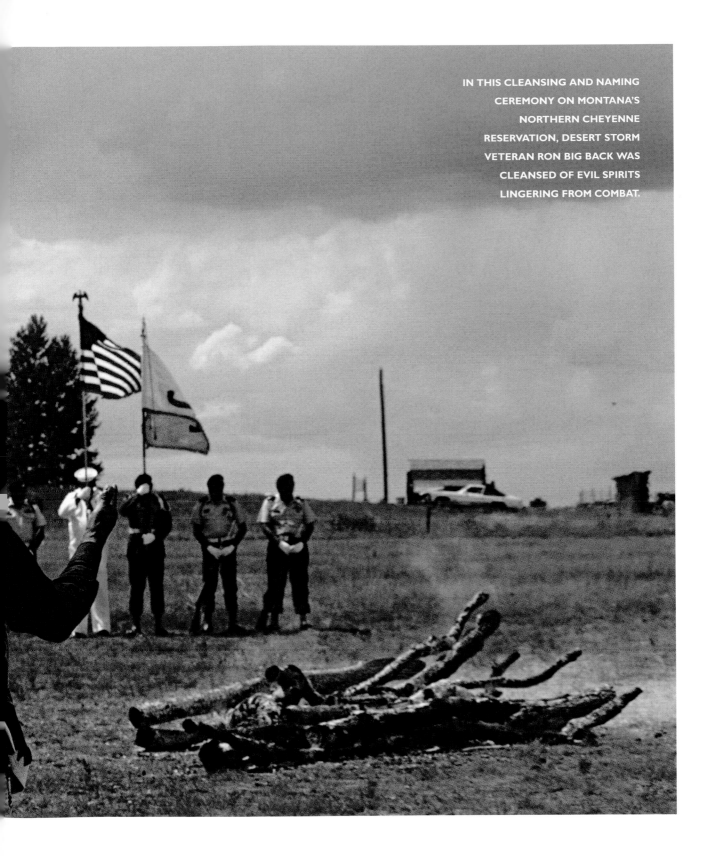

IN THIS CLEANSING AND NAMING CEREMONY ON MONTANA'S NORTHERN CHEYENNE RESERVATION, DESERT STORM VETERAN RON BIG BACK WAS CLEANSED OF EVIL SPIRITS LINGERING FROM COMBAT.

"The Sioux Got the Glory, the Crows Got the Land, but the Cheyenne Did the Fighting."

and two brothers. But this time luck ran out for him. Four months after arriving in Vietnam he was killed in action while trying to carry a wounded soldier to safety. Poolaw had four sons. Each entered the Army, and three served in Vietnam.

Another Plains Indian tribe that has revitalized its warrior traditions is the Northern Cheyenne Nation of Montana. The Cheyenne were one of the premier warrior peoples of the northern plains. Indeed, there is a popular saying in Indian country about Custer's Last Stand that expresses well the role of the Cheyenne on the battlefields of the American West: "The Sioux got the glory, the Crows got the land, but the Cheyenne did the fighting." For its tenacious resistance to westward expansion the tribe paid a terrible price in blood and tears. It still feels the effects of the government's relentless efforts to curb the warrior spirit. Nonetheless, its young men and women have been well represented in the armed forces of the United States since the end of the Indian wars.

CHEYENNE CEREMONIES

One of its modern-day warriors is Ron Big Back, a veteran of Desert Storm, the conflict that set the stage for the Iraq War a decade later. While in Kuwait, Army Private Big Back had had a frightening dream: He was riding a beautiful spotted horse and he was dressed as a traditional Cheyenne warrior. He and his horse came to a river and the horse splashed into it without hesitation. The water got deeper and the horse began swimming, and as the horse struggled across it

was beset by many poisonous snakes that bit it repeatedly. Although gravely hurt, the horse managed to reach the far bank, but it then collapsed and died. Big Back was able to step ashore unhurt, but he grieved for his fallen horse. What, he wondered, could the dream mean?

Worried, he wrote to his father, who showed the letter to Tom Rock Roads, a Vietnam veteran and a respected spiritual leader on the Northern Cheyenne Reservation. Rock Roads had a ready explanation: Ron Big Back was coping with evil spirits in Kuwait and would need a cleansing ceremony as soon as he returned. Rock Roads, a combat veteran himself, would perform the ceremony.

Meanwhile, another letter arrived from Kuwait, this one from Big Back's commanding officer telling the family that their son had performed heroically in the face of a Scud missile attack: Private Big Back had been on guard duty one night when a missile exploded near his position. At the time it was believed that Scud missiles spread harmful biological and chemical contaminants upon exploding. But ignoring the threat to his own safety, Private Big Back had alerted his sleeping comrades with a Cheyenne war cry and rushed to put out the ensuing fire.

When Big Back returned from Kuwait in May 1991, his family decided to conduct a ceremony confirming the revival and continuation of centuries-old traditions in which war heroes received the praise and plaudits of friends and relatives.

Some hundred people attended the ceremony including Austin Two Moons, whose

Ron Big Back receives a coup stick at his cleansing and naming ceremony. The stick is adorned with a simulated scalp lock.

grandfather fought Custer at the Little Big-horn, and Ben Nighthorse Campbell, then a congressman from Colorado.

Also present was the Northern Cheyenne Honor Guard, each representing branches of the U.S. armed forces, and a drum group. Arrayed in front of the emcee's lectern was a complete Iraqi soldier's uniform, including the boots, that Private Big Back had appropriated while serving in Kuwait.

Before the ceremony began, Big Back's father read the letter commending his son for bravery. The effort was almost too much for him and he began to cry. "Thank you so much for coming to witness this," he said. "I am so proud of my son.

I am so proud to know that he is a Cheyenne warrior like his ancestors."

Private Big Back first underwent a purification ceremony with the incense of sage to cleanse him of any evil spirits that lingered around him after his combat experience. Tom Rock Roads performed the ceremony, assisted by his friend Jimmy Red Cloud. Then Rock Roads gave Ron Big Back a new name, Charging Eagle. As part of the cleansing and naming ceremony, Rock Roads used a coup stick adorned with a simulated scalp lock, representing a scalp he had taken in Vietnam.

At the conclusion of the ceremony, Rock Roads presented Charging Eagle to his family and friends as the drummers and singers heralded him with a warrior's honor song. Then, taking charcoal from a large bonfire, Charging Eagle blessed and smudged the faces of each of the spectators, who helped themselves from the large pile of cloth, blankets, packaged goods, and other items the family had assembled for the giveaway in his honor.

The ceremony ended with a scalp dance led by Rock Roads and Charging Eagle accompanied by the Northern Cheyenne Honor Guard, who led the spectators around the bonfire and past the Iraqi uniform spread out on the ground in the dance area.

Each of the women picked up a stick from a nearby pile and used it to strike the uniform—"to count coup" on the symbolic Iraqi soldier—

as they danced past. All the while, the honor guard fired off rounds of blank ammunition from their rifles and the women burst forth with spontaneous trilling. A sudden thunder and lightning storm put out the fire and sent everyone rushing to their cars.

An elderly Cheyenne woman who was later asked if she had been present at the Big Back ceremony said no, but she had heard about it. She said it was good to know that some of the old-time ceremonies were coming back. The last time this ceremony had been performed, she believed, was after the Second World War. "I tell you," she laughed, "it was really something to see those old ladies dancing with those German and Japanese scalps!"

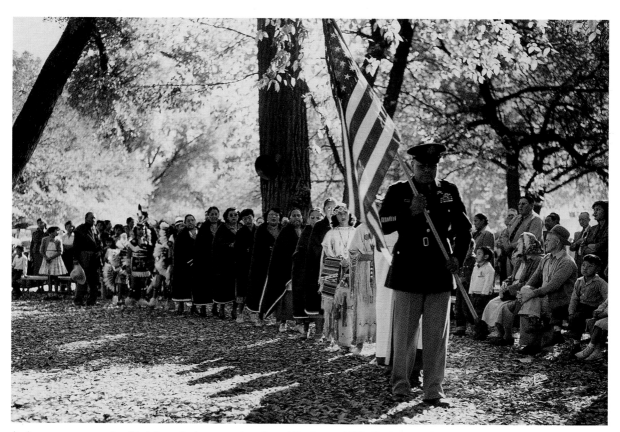

An honor ceremony for Black Legs Society member Pascal Poolaw in 1952. Poolaw would later be killed in Vietnam.

WARRIORS IN UNIFORM

She Said It Was Good to Know that Some of the Old-Time Ceremonies Were Coming Back.

CROW CEREMONIES

Adjoining the Northern Cheyenne Reservation is the Crow Reservation. Like their Cheyenne neighbors, the Crow also honor their veterans with celebrations and ceremonies. For example, when Crow soldiers returned to the reservation after World War II, their relatives would stage a welcome right at the train station and a week or two later hold a reception.

As World War II veteran Joseph Medicine Crow (see Chaper 4) recalled in *Counting Coup,* his welcome home reception in January 1946 was particularly memorable because he missed the gala at the Lodge Grass, Montana, train station.

En route his train stopped in Sheridan, Wyoming, for about a half hour, so he took the opportunity to buy a hamburger at a favored diner. "Louie could make a dime hamburger taste like a New York-cut sirloin," Medicine Crow recalls. "Boy, I sure missed those hamburgers while I was overseas."

Because of the detour, he missed the train and the large crowd waiting to welcome him. "My mother was ready with a stack of new Pendleton blankets to spread from the train to the singers, some 60 feet away," he remembers.

As Medicine Crow got off the train at Lodge Grass, he says, "I was supposed to walk along the row of blankets and start dancing as I reached the singers. Well, this didn't take place. . . . Poor Mom, she sure must have been disappointed."

As a result, Medicine Crow had to wait for his reception, which was held that weekend at the tribal dance hall in Lodge Grass. "As I walked into the hall," he recalls,

people along the way shook my hands, relatives hugged me, and admiring girls kissed me. . . . The drummers [then] sang the war honor song of my grandfather Chief Medicine Crow. I danced around the floor with my relatives dancing behind me.

Medicine Crow was then asked by some of the elders at the reception to tell everyone his combat experiences. He recalled being taken aback by the request, saying, "I had never thought about my activities on the battlefield as 'war deeds,' except when I captured the horses." He says,

I told the elders about my hand-to-hand encounter with the German soldier and how I took his gun away from him. Then I related the time I was in charge of the detail of soldiers that went after dynamite so the big guns along the Siegfried line could be blasted. And I told them about sneaking into the German camps and stealing the horses belonging to the SS officers. For those four coups, I was declared a full-fledged Crow war chief.

After the recitation of his war deeds, Medicine Crow's family started a giveaway, which is done to honor someone in Crow society. "I know in white society when someone is honored that person gets the presents," Medicine Crow says,

but that is not the way it is done in Crow society. When someone succeeds, he or she gives presents to those who helped

"The Words in My Honor Song...Reflect the Pride We Crow People Cherish...for Our Warrior Heroes."

make that success possible, like . . . relatives, teachers, and friends. My mother gave away a stack of new Pendleton blankets, quilts, and other nice things.

Medicine Crow's father gave away a horse with a new saddle and bridle. The giveaway was followed by a feast.

At the welcome home reception, Medicine Crow was given the name High Bird, after a warrior from the Whistling Water clan, and given his right to be a camp crier, or announcer. He also had an honor song composed for him:

High Bird, you are a great soldier!
High Bird, you fought the mighty Germans!
High Bird, you counted coup on them!
High Bird, you are a great soldier!

Medicine Crow uses his honor song in tribal ceremonies. "When it is played, I dance and my relatives follow me. The words in my honor song, like the songs of the Crow chiefs before me, reflect the pride we Crow people cherish to this day for our warrior heroes."

When Private Medicine Crow returned home from Germany he arrived by train. Sixty years later, Crow veterans are met at the airport. Otherwise little has changed. Typical is the reception accorded Marine Cpl. Ivan Wilson, who returned home on leave after serving seven months as part of Operation Iraqi Freedom (see page 204).

Three months earlier, less than 500 miles away in the little Pine Ridge Reservation town of Kyle, South Dakota, there had been another

honor ceremony for a Marine corporal, but this one was as sad as the other was joyous.

The returning Marine was Brett Lundstrom, the first Oglala Sioux fatality of Operation Iraqi Freedom. A procession also marked his return. At first it consisted only of a hearse, two vans with 12 Marines in dress uniform, and a police escort, but as it wound its way to the middle of the reservation, it continued to grow as cars and pickup trucks parked along the road took their place at the end of the line.

The procession stopped where a dozen or so horsemen, several wearing eagle feather war bonnets, waited alongside the road with a small empty horse-drawn wagon. After lifting the flag-draped casket from the hearse and placing it gently on the bed of the old wagon, the Marines stood at attention. At the command of one of the riders, the procession set off. The saddle of the last horse was empty.

Upon reaching the Little Wound High School, the Marines carried the flag-draped casket into the gymnasium and placed it before a 30-foot-tall tepee at one end of the hardwood floor. Then, beginning a rotation that would last for two days and nights, two Marines positioned themselves at opposite ends of the opened casket.

Seated in the gymnasium were friends and relatives of Lundstrom's family as well as numerous Lakota veterans who had come to honor the fallen warrior. Most of the veterans were wearing their service caps and uniforms, many of them emblazoned with unit patches, ribbons, and medals. Tucked into some of the caps was a single eagle feather.

Chris Lively, severely wounded while serving in Iraq, is an enthusiastic moccasin maker for Project Moccasin, which carries on the traditional practice.

Like Ivan Wilson, his Crow comrade in arms, Brett Lundstrom boasted a distinguished warrior heritage. Ironically, his ancestors often earned their warrior status fighting the Crow, once the mortal enemies of the Lakota. One of his distant relatives was Iron Hail, also known as Dewey Beard, who fought against Goes Ahead and Custer in the Battle of the Little Bighorn. Another ancestor was the great Lakota leader Red Cloud. Now, though, the Crow and Lakota are on the same side. One of Lundstrom's uncles was killed at the Battle of the Bulge during World War II. Another uncle died in Korea. His father, Ed Lundstrom, had recently retired from the Marines. Brett served three months in Afghanistan in 2004, before going to Iraq, where he was killed by small-arms fire in Fallujah. Corporal Lundstrom was 22.

The *Rocky Mountain News,* which covered the ceremony, reported that John Around Him, who emceed the ceremony for Lundstrom, explained, "Brett earns the American flag from his government. From his people, he earns the eagle feather," a tribal badge of honor for military service.

That night Corporal Lundstrom, who had never lived on the reservation—because his father was stationed elsewhere during his military career—was given a new name by his great-uncle, Birgil Kills Straight. As the *Rocky Mountain News* reported, Kills Straight explained the name's significance: "Before he enters the spirit world, it's important for him to have an Indian name, because that's how the ancestors will know him."

WARRIORS IN UNIFORM

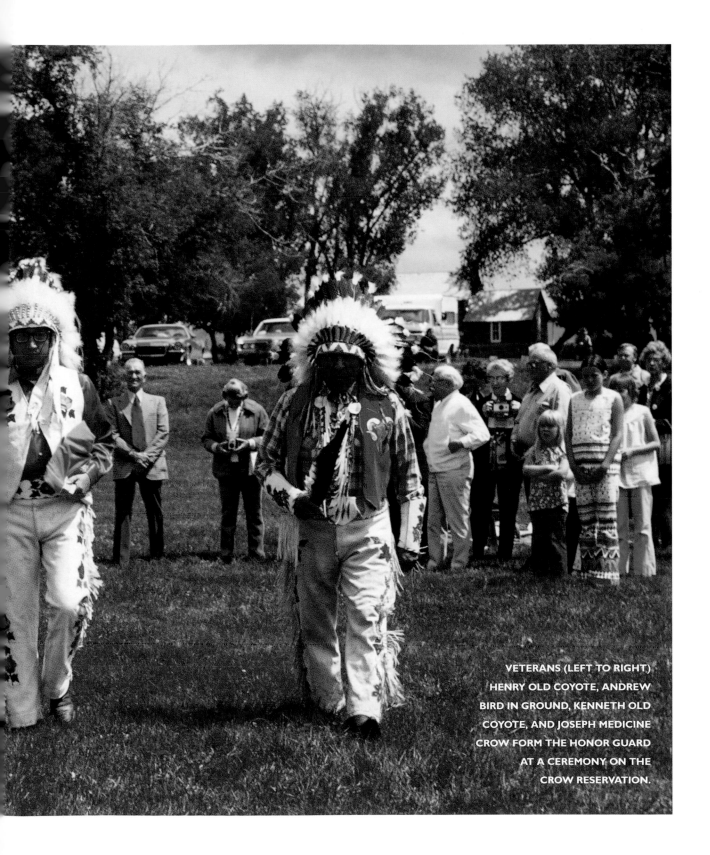

VETERANS (LEFT TO RIGHT)
HENRY OLD COYOTE, ANDREW
BIRD IN GROUND, KENNETH OLD
COYOTE, AND JOSEPH MEDICINE
CROW FORM THE HONOR GUARD
AT A CEREMONY ON THE
CROW RESERVATION.

The name Lundstrom received was Wanbli Isnala, or Lone Eagle, because, as Kills Straight explained, placing the eagle feather on Lundstrom's chest, "He, alone, above everything else, is an eagle. He will fly to the highest reaches of the universe. He may bring back news to us in our dreams."

Besides their ceremonies to help fallen warriors on their way to the afterlife, American Indian cultures also had ceremonies to help warriors who returned home injured in mind or spirit. These ceremonies helped bring the lives of their loved ones back into balance, enabling them to live again in peace and harmony, to be spiritually, emotionally, and mentally healthy. Such ceremonies are still integral to Native American cultural life. They are powerful, and they have helped many returning soldiers make an easier adjustment to civilian life than has been the experience of their non-Native comrades in arms. The Navajo, for example, have several such ceremonies. Their goal is to help war veterans return to a state of balance within the universe, *Hozho*.

PUEBLOAN CEREMONIES

Not all tribes glorify warfare, even though they honor their soldiers. For some, especially the Pueblo peoples of the Southwest, there is conflict between being a soldier and the possibility of taking another human's life.

This was well expressed in a 2003 interview in the *Arizona Republic* with Cliff Qotsaquahu,

An eagle feather was placed on the body of Cpl. Brett Lundstrom during the naming ceremony that prepared him properly for his journey into the afterlife.

WARRIORS IN UNIFORM

"How Can I Blend the White Man's Military Purpose with the Hopi Culture?"

then commander of American Legion Hopi Post 80. "Hopis are very reserved in talking about their combat experiences," he said. "They think, 'How can I be a good Hopi, knowing I possibly killed somebody, or did kill somebody? How can I blend the White man's military purpose with the Hopi culture?'" Traditional ceremonies, he said, provide a measure of solace.

In the cleansing ceremony, Qotsaquahu explained, the veteran's paternal aunts escort him into the village, where they wash his hair and give him a new name. Cleansing ceremonies of up to four days are also performed by spiritual leaders. But, Qotsaquahu said, "there are no statues among the Hopi for those killed in combat. We don't memorialize them. We believe that they have joined the Cloud People Society and that someday we will join them."

MAKING MOCCASINS

Another cultural practice modified by the realities of Indian life in the 21st century is the making of moccasins. Traditionally, a warrior went into battle wearing new moccasins made for him by one of his loved ones—a grandmother, a mother, a sister, a wife. The new moccasins were to see the warrior home safely from battle or ease his transition into the spirit world.

This practice continues in Project Moccasin, although its volunteers often have no idea who will receive the fruits of their labors. Sponsored by the National Native American Veterans Association of Oklahoma City and the American Indian Chamber of Commerce of Oklahoma, Project Moccasin was initiated by Anthony DeClue, a Lakota veteran living in St. Cloud, Minnesota, who is one of the moccasin makers. "I spent seven years in the Special Forces and I was disconnected from my heritage," DeClue explained to the *Native American Times*:

> I want the warriors in Afghanistan and Iraq to feel connected. When they take off their boots and put their feet in the moccasins they might feel a little closer to where they are from. What I do is thread them up. Another guy does the leatherwork—he stamps the leather with eagle feathers and sends it to me and I start painting them. The moccasins are smudged and we put a dream catcher and a piece of Mother Earth in each one so that our warriors will come home.

Another of the moccasin makers is Sgt. Chris Lively, an Army specialist who lives in Charlotte, Texas, with his wife and five children.

For Lively the project is especially meaningful because he is one of the Native soldiers who almost did not make it back from Iraq, suffering life-threatening injuries twice on the same day. He was riding in a vehicle that hit an improvised explosive device made of four 155 mortar rounds wired together with additional explosives. Fifteen minutes later, while chasing the insurgents who had exploded the first IED, his vehicle hit a 500-pound bomb that had failed to explode on impact and was recovered by the insurgents.

Sergeant Lively suffered a broken neck and other injuries that left him 100 percent disabled.

KIOWA BLACK LEGGINGS SOCIETY

After the invocation, the American flag is lowered to half-mast. The announcer starts to call the names of the deceased society members, all military veterans. This is only my second time at the Kiowa Black Leggings ceremonial, and I don't know any of the veterans whose names are called. But as the announcer continues, I can't help feeling a bit emotional as I listen to the fate of each deceased veteran—the words "killed while in captivity," "killed in action," and "body never recovered" send a chill through me.

But the words that truly bring a lump to my throat are "forever 19 years of age" or "forever 21 years of age," reminding me just how young these Kiowa soldiers were. As the list of deceased veterans is at last completed, the flag is raised and the dance continues.

The Ton-Kon-Ga, known as the Kiowa Black Leggings ceremonial, is held in May and October at Indian City near Anadarko, Oklahoma. The Ton-Kon-Ga is an old military society founded in the 19th century, in the days when the Kiowa fought other Native nations for hunting territory, and also fought the encroachment of the non-Native into their territory. It is unknown as to how the society received its name. Some believe that the name honors Kiowa warriors who survived an enemy attack during battle, in which prairie grasses were set on fire. Today, the Black Leggings Society honors the military service of its members. For a visitor attending the dance for the first time, it might seem unusual to see American flags and military insignias throughout the camp area, considering the historical treatment of the Kiowa by the United States government.

Once young Kiowa men have enlisted into military service, though, the American flag and military insignias become an important symbol of their service. Honoring the accomplishment of their warriors has long been a tradition among the Kiowa people. War deeds have been remembered through songs, painted on tepees, drawn in ledger books, and recorded on hide or muslin in the form of a calendar of events called a winter count.

One unusual tradition that has continued is the performance of the scalp and victory dances; these are done by the female family members of the veterans. The women dance wearing eagle-feather headdresses and carrying lances of their male

At a Black Leggings ceremonial a woman dances in a dress of traditional black and red cloth and carries a traditional lance.

relatives. This is an opportunity for them to appropriately salute the military accomplishments of the veterans, since it would not be considered proper for them to brag. The women also wear dresses made of red and black cloth, which symbolize the blood that was spilled in battle and the deaths that occurred. The passion displayed by the women is thrilling: Dancing vigorously, they shake their lances, while the voices of the singers mix with the trilling of the women's voices and the sound of the drum.

Once the women are finished, the male members of the society enter the dance arena singing unaccompanied. The members of the society are garbed in red capes, representing a captured war trophy from a battle with the Mexican army. Military patches displaying rank and branch of service are sewn to the capes. As they continue their entrance, the singers take over, accompanied by the drum. I don't have to understand the Kiowa words of the song to know how powerful it is.

In the Ton-Kon-Ga, there are two special positions held by young boys. Each is called Aw-Day-Tah-Lee (much-honored son). As I read the account of the Aw-Day-Tah-Lee in the magazine *Whispering Wind* given by Vanessa Jennings, a Kiowa beadworker and cradleboard maker, I understood why these two positions were so highly respected by the Kiowa people. Jennings says:

War bonnets adorn uniform jackets, an appropriate blending of two cultures and the warrior tradition that is so much a part of both worlds.

> In one tribal memory, a group of Kiowas had gone on a raid. They ran into trouble and were cornered in an unexpected skirmish with battle-seasoned soldiers who had plenty of ammunition. The Kiowas were pinned down. If they stayed, they would all be killed. The decision was made by the leader to get the horses and make for freedom. The warriors had left their horses in the care of a quiet and attentive boy. The leader signaled for the boy to bring all of the horses

immediately. I can imagine the surprise of the soldiers when they saw this exquisite ten year old riding fearlessly into the middle of this fire fight leading the horses. . . . The shouts and the bullets fell in a dangerous hail around that little boy as he held onto his mount and drove the horses past the soldiers and into the waiting hands of the Kiowas. I can see the tender care given that child's body as the Kiowas escaped. They made sure they did not leave him behind after that valiant act to save his fellow warriors.

—Emil Her Many Horses

THE RETURN CEREMONY FOR MARINE CPL. IVAN WILSON

When 23-year-old Marine Cpl. Ivan Wilson, a member of the Crow Nation, descended the stairs into the terminal at Logan International Airport in Billings, Montana, in April 2006, he was accorded a warrior's welcome in a modern context. Awaiting him was a crowd of nearly 100 relatives, tribal members, and a drum group wearing eagle-feather headdresses and beaded vests. At the bottom of the steps stood his father with a bouquet of balloons in one hand and framed photographs of his son's warrior ancestors in the other.

Wilson stood at attention as a fellow tribal veteran placed a war bonnet on his head, beginning a ceremony that featured praise songs and chants, warrior dances, and a procession around the terminal. Many of his Crow family members and friends carried American flags and wore T-shirts and shawls bearing his photograph and the Marine Corps insignia. Typical of the Crow women's welcome for returning warriors, the shawls had earlier been spread out on the lobby floor as Wilson made his descent of the stairway. "I'm excited, I'm happy, and I'm proud," his mother, Carol White Clay, told the *Billings Gazette*.

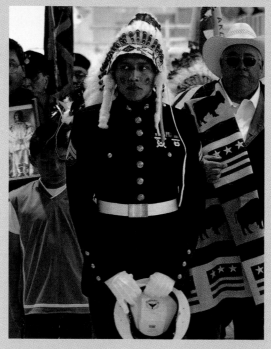

Cpl. Ivan Wilson was honored following his return from Iraq.

At the conclusion of the ceremony, Burton Pretty on Top, speaking for the family, told the fascinated throng of travelers and airport personnel, "What you have witnessed was a young man honored in the Crow traditional way."

Wilson, who served as a military police officer at Camp Fallujah in Iraq, has a distinguished warrior heritage. One of his relatives was Goes Ahead, a scout for the Seventh Cavalry at the Battle of the Little Bighorn. Another was Big Shoulderblade, a pipe carrier in Crow war parties led by Plenty Coups. The last war chief of the Crow, Plenty Coups spoke at the dedication of the Tomb of the Unknown Soldier at Arlington Cemetery. Wilson's grandfather, Raymond Bear Below, served with the U.S. Army in both World War II and Korea. Before his death in 1997, Bear Below often expressed the wish that his grandson would also join the military. Ivan Wilson was happy to honor his grandfather's wish. "I've just always believed that Indians should be warriors. I wanted to support my wife and kids and give them something to look up to, and that's what I work to do every day."

"We May Have Been a Conquered People, but We Were Not a Defeated People."

Nonetheless, he is able to make moccasins and is one of Project Moccasin's most enthusiastic supporters. In fact, he made one pair of moccasins for Sgt. Chuck Boers. Like so many of the Indians in the military, Lively sees himself as a soldier carrying on a warrior tradition. As part of a nine-person team—a modern-day "war party" —he helped capture three insurgents who had killed 14 Iraqi soldiers. "If you can count coup by taking away an enemy's weapon, then I did this," he says. During his entire time in Iraq, Lively carried a medicine bundle. His only regret was not having a bow and arrows with him. "I am very much into archery and I think if I had been able to take my bow and arrows to Iraq, it would have frightened the insurgents."

Lively grew up not knowing much about his Indian heritage. He was born in Washington, D.C., but his mother gave him up for adoption. He did not learn that he was part Iroquois, Apache, and Cherokee until he was almost grown. His mother was Iroquois and Cherokee, his father part Apache. Lively says,

Once I did know, I grasped my heritage with relish, learning as much as I could about who I am and who my people were. I took that with me to Iraq. The skills I learned came in useful in the desert badlands—the ability to pick out the bad guys in a crowd, the ability to see hidden explosive devices when hardly a track was made. Indians have a natural sense, almost like ESP. Maybe it is in our DNA. I don't want to exaggerate, but it is an unexplainable heightened sense of surroundings, an awareness, that spooks non-Indians. For example, during one of my missions in Iraq I had a terrible sense of foreboding, that something was wrong. I told the driver to stop. I was the gunner. Just as we stopped an IED exploded directly in front of us.

Besides serving in Iraq, Lively was with the Fifth Special Forces in Libya and with the Seventh Special Forces in Colombia. He says,

I was in Libya when they bombed [leader Muammar Qaddafi], and a year later, in 87, I was in the jungles fighting the Drug Lords in Operation Snow Cap. In Libya I was shot, in Colombia I was stabbed, and I was hit by the two IED's in Iraq, but I was proud to be a soldier and I am proud to be an American Indian. We are and have always been a vital asset to the military and other law enforcement agencies. Although we are still considered "injuns" and called "chief" and other derogatory names, we don't complain. We are still proud and we hold our heads up high as we have throughout history. But the fact that American Indians are fighting for this great country of ours needs to be recognized. We may have been a conquered people, but we were not a defeated people, and our warriors will always rise to the call of battle.

WILLIAM UNDER BAGGAGE, WHOSE NEPHEW CPL. BRETT LUNDSTROM WAS KILLED IN IRAQ, HOLDS A PHOTOGRAPH OF THE SOLDIER DURING HIS WAKE.

NAVY KIVA

This painting, by Navajo artist Virgil Nez, represents a ship sailing into the sun and honors Nez's uncle, Pete Clah, who served in the U.S. Navy during World War II.

Happily may their roads back home be on the trail of pollen.

Happily may they all get back.

In beauty I walk.

With beauty before me, I walk.

With beauty behind me, I walk.

With beauty below me, I walk.

With beauty above me, I walk.

With beauty all around me, I walk.

It is finished in beauty,

It is finished in beauty,

It is finished in beauty,

It is finished in beauty.

'Sa'ah naaghéi, Bik'eh hózhó
—from a Navajo Ceremony

BIBLIOGRAPHY

Ball, Eve. *In the Days of Victorio: Recollections of a Warm Springs Apache.* University of Arizona Press, 1970.

Benton, Kenneth L. "Warrior From West Point." *Soldiers Magazine*, February 1974.

Benzel, Lance. "Crow ceremony marks Marine's return from Iraq." *Billings Gazette*, April 12, 2006.

Bernstein, Alison R. *American Indians and World War II: Toward a New Era in Indian Affairs.* University of Oklahoma Press, 1991.

Bierhorst, John , ed. *Four Masterworks of American Indian Literature: Quetzelcoatl, the Ritual of Condolence, Cuceb, the Night Chant.* University of Arizona Press, 1974.

Britten, Thomas A. *American Indians in World War I: At War and at Home.* University of New Mexico Press, 1997.

Dippie, Brian W. *The Vanishing Indian: White Attitudes and U.S. Indian Policy.* Wesleyan University Press, 1982.

Dunlay, Thomas W. *Wolves for the Blue Soldiers: Indian Scouts and Auxiliaries with United States Army*, 1860-90. University of Nebraska Press, 1982.

Franco, Jere' Bishop. *Crossing the Pond: The Native American Effort in World War II.* University of North Texas Press, 1999.

Gibson, Daniel. "Desert Thunder: Powwow in Iraq." *Native Peoples Magazine*, March/April 2005.

Graman, Kevin. "Healing path from Vietnam a twisted trail." *Spokesman-Review*, June 25, 2005.

Hauptman, Laurence M. *Between Two Fires: American Indians in the Civil War.* University of New Mexico Press, 1997.

Healy, Donald T., and Peter J. Orenski. *Native American Flags.* University of Oklahoma Press, 2003.

Holm, Tom. *Strong Hearts, Wounded Souls: Native American Veterans of the Vietnam War.* University of Texas Press, 1996.

Langellier, John P. *American Indians in the U.S. Armed Forces, 1866-1945.* The G.I. Series: The Illustrated History of the American Soldier, His Uniform and His Equipment. Greenhill Books and Stackpole Books, 2000.

Linderer, Gary A. *Eyes of the Eagle: F Comany LRPs in Vietnam, 1968.* Ballantine Books, 1991.

Medicine Crow, Joseph. *Counting Coup: Becoming a Crow Chief on the Reservation and Beyond.* The National Geographic Society, 2006.

Nichols, Judy. "Native Americans Have Noteworthy War Record," *Arizona Republic*, March 23, 2003.

"Project Moccasins," *Native American Times*, April 19, 2995.

Roosevelt, Theodore. *The Rough Riders* Charles Scribner's Sons, 1899.

———. *The Winning of the West.* University of Nebraska Press, 1995.

Sheeler, Jim. "Wake for an Indian Warrior." *Rocky Mountain News*, January 21, 2006.

Tate, Michael L. "Soldiers of the Line: Apache Companies in the U.S. Army, 1891-1897. *Arizona and the West*, 16 (Winter 1974).

Townsend, Kenneth Williams. *World War II and the American Indian.* University of New Mexico Press, 2000.

Viola, Herman J. *After Columbus: The Smithsonian Chronicle of the North American Indians.* Smithsonian Institution Press, 1990.

White, Willliam B. *The Military and the Melting Pot: The American Army and Minority Groups, 1865-1894.* Ph.D. dissertation. University of Wisconsin, 1968.

ACKNOWLEDGMENTS

The author wishes to thank:

Gen. Gordon Sullivan, Lt. Gen. Ted Stroup, and Ann Belyae, Association of the United States Army; Sgt. Chuck Boers, U.S. Army; Lt. Col. Mark A. Smith, U.S.M.A., West Point; Suzan Shown Harjo, The Morning Star Institute; Dr. Tim McCleary, Little Bighorn Community College; Chief Larry D. Nichols, Lower Muskogee/Creek Nation; Emil Her Many Horses and Dr. George P. Horse Capture, National Museum of the Ameridan Indian; Dr. Joseph Medicine Crow and Carson Walks Over Ice, Crow Nation; James Cates, National Native American Veterans Association; Dr. B. Byron Price; Director, University of Oklahoma Press; Michael E. Gonzales; Bob Weis; Robert Johnson; Gordon McLester, Oneida Nation; the Emhoolah Family, Kiowa Nation; Debbie Sankey, Toy Kelley; Joyce Mathews; Nancy Tsoodle; Gary D. Kodaseet; Bill Howell; Tom Knife Chief, James Elsberry, Mark Ellenbarger.

CONTRIBUTORS

Master Sgt. Johan Charles Boers, an enrolled member of the Lipan, Apache, has been in the U.S. Army for over 25 years.

Ben Nighthorse Campbell is a former senator and congressman from Colorado. A member of the Northern Cheyenne Nation, he was the only Native American in the U. S. Congress during his political career.

Suzan Shown Harjo (Cheyenne and Muscogee), a writer, curator, and policy advocate, has developed federal Indian policy since 1975, including the National Museum of the American Indian Act.

Emil Her Many Horses (Oglala Lakota) is an associate curator for the National Museum of the American Indian in Washington, D.C., since 1998. Emil is a traditional artist specializing in Lakota beadwork and dolls.

Toy McKinley Kelly, an enrolled member of the Osage Nation, works for the Departments of History and Political Science at the University of Tulsa. She has served as president of the state chapter of American War Mothers and is currently its treasurer.

Joseph Medicine Crow is the author of several books on Crow history and culture and is an adviser to the National Museum of the American Indian and the Buffalo Bill Historical Center.

Lt. Col. Mark Smith is a professor at the U.S. Military Academy, West Point, and officer in charge of the Native American Club. On his father's side he is a descendent of the Allen Family of the Cherokees of South Carolina. On his mother's side he is a descendant of the Muscogee (Creek) and Choctaw.

Marine Master Gunnery Sgt. Vernon Tsoodle, having served two tours in Korea and Vietnam, is one of the Kiowa tribe's elite warriors and a member of the Oklahoma Military Hall of Fame.

Carson Walks Over Ice, a veteran of the Vietnam War, is director of the Crow Indian Veterans Project. He serves in the tribe's Honor Guard, is a drummer and singer, and is active in promoting and preserving Crow history and culture.

ILLUSTRATIONS CREDITS

2-3, Library of Congress; 6, Peter Turnley/CORBIS; 8, Chuck Boers; 15, Courtesy Jon Malinowski; 16-17, The Granger Collection, NY; 18, George Romney/The Bridgeman Art Library/Getty Images; 20, Herman J. Viola Collection; 21, Special Collections, Harvey A. Andruss Library/Bloomsburg University of Pennsylvania; 22-23, Library of Congress; 25 Art Resource, NY; 26, Herman J. Viola Collection; 27, Library of Congress; 28, The Granger Collection, NY; 29, The Granger Collection, NY; 30, Herman J. Viola Collection; 31, National Museum of the American Indian, Smithsonian Institution; 33, Courtesy of The North Carolina State Archives; 34-35, MPI/Getty Images; 37, Wisconsin Historical Society; 38, Herman J. Viola Collection; 39 (UP), Herman J. Viola Collection; 39 (MID), Herman J. Viola Collection; 39 (LO), Herman J. Viola Collection; 40-41, National Museum of the American Indian, Smithsonian Institution; 42, National Museum of the American Indian, Smithsonian Institution; 44, Denver Public Library, Western History Collection; 46-47, Library of Congress; 48, Library of Congress; 49, Edwin L. Wisherd; 50-51, The Picture Desk; 52, National Archives and Records Administration; 53, National Archives and Records Administration; 54-55, Courtesy Arizona Historical Society; 57, Library of Congress; 58, National Museum of the American Indian, Smithsonian Institution; 60, Denver Public Library, Western History Collection; 61, Library of Congress; 62, Milwaukee Public Museum; 63 (UP), Milwaukee Public Museum; 64 (LO), Milwaukee Public Museum; 65-66, Wisconsin Historical Society; 67, Indiana University Mathers Library Wanamaker Collection; 68, Courtesy Karl May Verlag; 69, Oklahoma Historical Society; 70-71, Indiana University Mathers Library Wanamaker Collection; 72, Oklahoma Historical Society; 73, Western History Collections, University of Oklahoma Libraries; 74, Timothy McCleary; 75, Indiana University Mathers Library Wanamaker Collection; 76, Al Abrams; 78-79, CORBIS; 80, Courtesy Jon Malinowski; 81, Seely G. Mudd Library, Princeton University; 82, National Museum of the American Indian, Smithsonian Institution; 83, (UP), National Museum of the American Indian, Smithsonian Institution; 83 (MID), National Museum of the American Indian, Smithsonian Institution; 83 (LO), National Museum of the American Indian, Smithsonian Institution; 84-85, Joe Rosenthal/AP/Wide World Photos; 86, AP/Wide World Photos; 89, National Archives and Records Administration; 91, Courtesy Suzan Harjo; 92-93, Seely G. Mudd Library, Princeton University; 94, U.S. Department of Defense/CNP/Getty Images; 95, National Archives and Records Administration; 96, National Archives and Records Administration; 97, Seely G. Mudd Library, Princeton University; 98, U.S. Army Signal Corps/AP/Wide World Photos; 99, Courtesy William Howell; 100, Chuck Boers; 103, National Archives and Records Administration; 104, CORBIS; 107, Seely G. Mudd Library, Princeton University; 108, CORBIS; 109, Courtesy William Howell; 111, Glen Swanson; 112, Library of Congress; 113 (UP), Library of Congress; 113 (LO), Library of Congress; 114-115, CORBIS; 116, AP/Wide World Photos; 118, National Archives and Records Administration; 119, National Archives and Records Administration; 121, 1st Lt. William Nichols/AP/Wide World Photos; 123, Courtesy Vernon Tsoodle; 124, Courtesy Bonnie Stephenson; 125, CORBIS; 126-127, AP/Wide World Photos; 128, Official U. S. Navy Photograph courtesy of the Cherokee Heritage Center, Tahlequah, Oklahoma; 130, Courtesy Vernon Tsoodle; 132, Courtesy Debbie Sankey; 134, The Harry S. Truman Presidential Library ; 136 (UP), Simon Roberts/Getty Images; 136 (LO), National Museum of the American Indian, Smithsonian Institution; 137 (UP), National Museum of the American Indian, Smithsonian Institution; 137 (LO), National Museum of the American Indian, Smithsonian Institution; 138-139, AP/Wide World Photos; 140, CORBIS; 143, Courtesy Teri Frazier; 145, The Minneapolis Institute of Arts; 146, Courtesy Vernon Tsoodle; 148-149, Herman J. Viola Collection; 150, Courtesy Vernon Tsoodle; 153 (UP), Herman J. Viola Collection; 153 (LO), Herman J. Viola Collection; 154, Courtesy James Chastain; 156, National Museum of the American Indian, Smithsonian Institution; 157 (UP), Courtesy Emil Her Many Horses; 157 (LO), Courtesy Emil Her Many Horses; 158-159, Military Times; 160, Chuck Boers; 163, Scott S. Warren/AURORA; 164-165, Chuck Boers; 166, Chuck Boers; 169, Chuck Boers; 170-171, Chuck Boers; 173, Chuck Boers; 174, Chuck Boers; 176-177, Chuck Boers; 179, Michael A. Casey; 180, Courtesy Vernon Tsoodle; 181 (LE), Glen Swanson; 181 (RT), Wisconsin Historical Society; 182-183, Robert van der Hilst/CORBIS; 184, Chuck Boers; 187, National Museum of the American Indian, Smithsonian Institution; 189, James Elsberry; 190-191, Herman J. Viola Collection; 193, Herman J. Viola Collection; 194, Courtesy Linda Poolaw; 197, Courtesy Chris Lively; 198-199, Herman J. Viola Collection; 200, Todd Heisler/Rocky Mountain News/Polaris; 202, Courtesy Emil Her Many Horses; 203, Courtesy Emil Her Many Horses; 204, Billings Gazette; 206-207, Todd Heisler/Rocky Mountain News/Polaris; 208, Virgil J. Nez, *http://www.virgiljnez.com/*.

INDEX

Warriors
IN UNIFORM

Herman J. Viola

Published by the National Geographic Society

John M. Fahey, Jr., President and Chief Executive Officer

Gilbert M. Grosvenor, Chairman of the Board

Tim T. Kelly, President, Global Media Group

John Q. Griffin, President, Publishing

Nina D. Hoffman, Executive Vice President;
    President, Book Publishing Group

Prepared by the Book Division

Kevin Mulroy, Senior Vice President and Publisher

Leah Bendavid-Val, Director of Photography
    Publishing and Illustrations

Marianne R. Koszorus, Director of Design

Barbara Brownell Grogan, Executive Editor

Elizabeth Newhouse, Director of Travel Publishing

Carl Mehler, Director of Maps

Staff for This Book

Judith Klein, Project Editor

Peggy Archambault, Art Director

Robert Waymouth, Illustrations Editor,
    Illustrations Specialist

Ric Wain, Production Project Manager

Linda Johansson, Design Assistant

Jennifer A. Thornton, Managing Editor

R. Gary Colbert, Production Director

Manufacturing and Quality Management

Christopher A. Liedel, Chief Financial Officer

Phillip L. Schlosser, Vice President

Chris Brown, Technical Director

Nicole Elliott, Manager

Monika D. Lynde, Manager

Rachel Faulise, Manager

Founded in 1888, the National Geographic Society is one of the largest nonprofit scientific and educational organizations in the world. It reaches more than 285 million people worldwide each month through its official journal, *National Geographic,* and its four other magazines; the National Geographic Channel; television documentaries; radio programs; films; books; videos and DVDs; maps; and interactive media. National Geographic has funded more than 8,000 scientific research projects and supports an education program combating geographic illiteracy.

For more information, please call 1-800-NGS LINE (647-5463) or write to the following address:

National Geographic Society
1145 17th Street N.W.
Washington, D.C. 20036-4688 U.S.A.

Visit us online at www.nationalgeographic.com/books

For information about special discounts for bulk purchases, please contact National Geographic Books Special Sales: ngspecsales@ngs.org

For rights or permissions inquiries, please contact National Geographic Books Subsidiary Rights: ngbookrights@ngs.org

Library of Congress
Cataloging-in-Publication Data
Viola, Herman J.
  Warriors in uniform : the legacy of American Indian heroism / by Herman J. Viola ; foreword by Carson Walks Over Ice ; introduction by Ben Nighthorse Campbell.
    p. cm.
  Includes bibliographical references and index.
ISBN 978-1-4262-0361-9 (trade)
  1. Indians of North America--Warfare. 2. World War, 1914-1918--Participation, Indian. 3. World War, 1939-1945--Participation, Indian. 4. Korean War, 1950-1953--Participation, Indian. 5. Vietnam War, 1961-1975--Participation, Indian. 6. Iraq War, 2003--Participation, Indian. I. Title.
E98.W2V56 2008
970.004'97--dc22
2008021390

Printed in China